Foreword

"Aspects of the Boer Horsemen," gives a reada historical background to Malcolm Archibald's Boer War trilogy, and explains how his inspiration started with the war diary of a relation, who was a Scottish soldier in the Boer War. This is reprinted in full here, and its expansion to a trilogy is an amazing creative and imaginative achievement.

Malcolm Archibald won the 2005 Dundee Book Prize, with a magnificent historical novel about Dundee and the whaling trade of the 19th century, *"Whales for the Wizard"* (Polygon)

His Boer War trilogy is equally gripping, bringing history to life. *"Soldier of the Queen," "Horseman of the Veldt"* and *"Selkirk of the Fethan"* are the three books of the trilogy.

Great reads – enjoy them.

Zander Wedderburn   *Fledgling Press*

Other books by Malcolm Archibald

Bridges, Islands and Villages of the Forth
(Lang Syne Press, 1990)

Scottish Battles
(Chambers, 1990)

Scottish Myths and Legends
(Chambers, 1992)

Scottish Animal and Bird Folklore
(St Andrew Press, 1996)

Sixpence for the Wind: A Knot of Nautical Folklore
(Whittles, 1999)

Across the Pond: Chapters From the Atlantic
(Whittles, 2001)

Soldier of the Queen
(Fledgling Press, 2003)

Winner of the 2005 Dundee Book Prize
Whales for the Wizard
(Polygon Press 2005)

Horseman of the Veldt and **Selkirk of the Fethan**
(Fledgling Press, 2005)

Mother Law: a parchment for Dundee
(Fledgling Press, 2006)

Aspects of the Boer War:

Boers and Horsemen:

by

Malcolm Archibald

© Copyright 2005 by Malcolm Archibald

Cover illustration by Keir Murdoch © Copyright 2003

ISBN 0 95 441214 1

Note: Every attempt has been made to be accurate in this historical account, and give proper references to sources used. Any errors are those of the author. The publisher and author would be delighted to receive any factual corrections.

Published by Fledgling Press 2005

Printed by Digisource GB Limited in Livingston, Scotland

iv

Aspects of the Boer War:

Boers and Horsemen

by

Malcolm Archibald

For Cathy

Acknowledgements

I would like to thank Rene McRobbie of the Argyll and Sutherland Highlanders Regimental Museum, The Castle, Stirling, for her assistance in providing information about Private Robert Brown and the Argylls in general. I would also like to thank the late Mr Douglas Doyle of Natal, South Africa, for providing information on his father, Major Richard Doyle and for his kind permission to use it, and my mother in law, Mrs Cathy Moffat of Gorebridge for allowing me to copy her uncle's journal in full.

Finally I would like to thank Cathy, my wife, and Alex and Hannah, for their patience when I lived inside the life of Drew Selkirk.

Malcolm Archibald   Dundee, April 2005

Contents

Introduction 1

Chapter 1 : The Road To War.................................... 3

Chapter 2 : The Boers.. 8

Chapter 3 : The British Army 22

Chapter 4 : Diary Of Pt. R. Brown No 4538 I A&SH. 26

Chapter 5 : Horsemen And Border Reivers........... 44

Chapter 6 : The Course Of The War 53

Chapter 7:'The Bleak Cruelty Of An Apathetic Parliament' ... 58

Chapter 8 :The Scottish Connection 66

Chapter 9 : The Boer System Of Fighting 71

Chapter 10 : Foreign Involvement.......................... 78

Chapter 11 : Help From The Colonies.................... 91

Chapter 12 : Horsemen Of The Veldt.................... 102

Chapter 13 : A Gathering Of Generals 120

Chapter 14 : A Brace Of Burghers......................... 133

Chapter 15 : The Black Peoples 141

Chapter 16 : Results Of The War............................ 145

Bibliography : Published 149

Non Published Sources 153

Introduction

In 2003 Fledgling Press published *Soldier of the Queen*, the first of a trilogy of novels set in the British- Boer War of 1899-1902. Since then a number of people suggested that it might be an idea to write a book setting the story in context and explaining some of the themes. The outcome was this volume. It is not an exhaustive history, but a selection of interrelated essays, or thematic chapters, which attempt to describe or examine various aspects of the war as experienced by Drew Selkirk, the main character of the trilogy. Although Selkirk is a fictitious character, many of the military adventures that Selkirk survived in *Soldier of the Queen* came from the diary of a genuine Scottish soldier. His name was Robert Brown, he served with the Argyll and Sutherland Highlanders and he was invalided home after suffering enteric fever in April 1900.

Private Brown came from Methil in Fife. It is unlikely that he was any better, or any worse than the average Scottish soldier who campaigned for Queen Victoria. As such his opinions and language can be taken as typical of his type. His family still live in Scotland; I have been married to his grand-niece for some twenty four years and his journal is reproduced in full in this book.

Selkirk, the irregular cavalryman, is a different animal. Although the government sent tens of thousands of infantrymen to South Africa, they eventually realised that it was a horse-soldier's war. Indeed it could be argued that the Second (or Third, if Harry Smith's victorious campaign at Boomplaats is considered) Boer War of 1899-1902 was the last ever war where cavalry played a major part. The vast distances, combined with the Boers' natural mobility, led to the latter stages being dominated by mounted commandos and British columns.

The British augmented their cavalry force with scores of small, irregular bands of horse. Some, such as Brabant's or Rimington's, numbered in the hundreds and became well known. Other units were much smaller, were often raised for a specific objective and often disappeared nearly as quickly as they were formed.

One of the most successful formations was named the Scottish Horse, or Tullibardine's Desperados, and was composed of Scots, South Africans and Australians. The Scottish Horse survived the war to fight in both World Wars and was not finally disbanded until 1956. Another, much smaller, formation was Doyle's Australian Scouts, which were attached to the staff of General Walter Kitchener and acted as scouts and bait to the main column. With the permission of his son, the late Douglas Doyle, many of Major Doyle's adventures and a description of his tactics have been included in a chapter of this book. To put Drew Selkirk in context, the book includes a chapter about the importance of the horse to the Scottish Borders. Other chapters deal with the background of the war, the Boer and British methods of combat, the horrors of the concentration camps, the international reaction to the war, the experiences of the black Africans and thumbnail sketches of some British generals and Boer commanders. Finally the war is put into the context of its time.

Chapter 1 : The Road To War

By 1899 Britain had painted her red empire across a quarter of the globe. From Canada to Cape Town, Antigua to Auckland, the Union Flag flapped in pride, secure in the protection of the largest navy in the world. Much of Britain's foreign policy was dominated by the need to maintain the sea-lanes to India, and, despite the opening of the Suez Canal in 1869, the route around the Cape of Good Hope was a life-line for trade.

British influence in India had steadily increased during the Eighteenth Century, but her prestige as a colonial power was diminished by defeat during the American Revolutionary War (1775 – 1783). However, the French Revolutionary War (1793 – 1801), followed quickly by the Napoleonic War (1803 – 1815) provided opportunities for recouping some of her losses by scooping up the possessions of her European enemies. When the Netherlands became an ally of France, Britain moved against the Dutch colonies and in 1795 occupied the southern tip of Africa, an excellent staging post on the long voyage to India. Although the Cape was returned during the brief peace of 1802, the resumption of war saw another British army land in 1806. This time the British remained, for at the peace of 1814 Britain bought Cape Colony from the Dutch for £6,000.000. However, the strategic, fertile colony that Britain had purchased contained a population that included many antagonistic elements, from the hunter-gathering San people, through the Khoikhoi, Sotho and Nguni to the Boers. The name given to these originally European people, Boer, reveals their lifestyle and occupation, for Boer means farmer.

The Boers were a vigorous, hybrid race, the product of early Dutch settlers mingled with German immigrants and French Huguenot refugees. They demanded only to be left in peace, and when the British brought in both settlers and new anti-slavery laws, many Boers bundled their possessions into ox-wagons and headed north. For upwards of a century they had been gradually expanding, with each succeeding generation pushing the frontier further forward to create farms in the interior. The imposition of British laws encouraged many to cross the Orange River and trek into the interior while others crossed the Drakensberg to Natal. They carved out their own lands, fighting hostile tribes with musket and the Bible. Despite the Boers' desire for independence, the British found it relatively easy to annex the coastal province of Natal, establishing a crown colony in 1843.

The Boers trekked again, to found the Orange Free State and the South African Republic. Within five years, Sir Harry Smith, a veteran of the Napoleonic War and now Governor of Cape Colony, had followed and annexed this new nation, but in 1852 the British government repudiated Smith's action and allowed the two Boer republics their independence. Although the small Boer nations maintained friendly relations with one another, they never merged into a single nation. The Boer character of prickly independence was not always an asset. In the meantime the British fought various frontier wars with the Bantu peoples of Xhosa and Basuto and extended an acquisitive hand when diamonds were discovered in Griqualand West. In theory the part white, part black Griquas were also independent, yet when the South African Republic claimed their land and the diamonds therein, Britain snatched neighbouring Basutoland and then, in 1877, declared that they also ruled the South African Republic.

In 1879, the Zulu War broke out, with the destruction of the 24th Foot at the battle of Isandlwana, being followed by the defence of Rorke's Drift and the final victory of Ulundi. Another two years passed before the South African Republic revolted against British rule and in an amazing sequence of skirmishes succeeded in throwing out the British. The most notable battle was fought at Majuba, which featured three warriors later to become famous: Ian Hamilton, Hector Macdonald and Christiaan De Wet. The Gordon Highlanders in particular remembered the defeat at Majuba.

Queen Victoria was not happy about Boer self-determination, for she did not approve of the manner in which the Boers treated the black African peoples, but notwithstanding Her Majesty's displeasure, the Republic regained its independence and in 1883 Paul Kruger became the president. The following year gold was unearthed in the Witwatersrand – the 'ridge of white waters' - that lay near to Pretoria in the southern Transvaal, as the South African Republic was becoming known. As so often in the 19th century, the discovery of gold led to massive immigration and thousands of prospectors destroyed the peace of the veldt. The majority of these were British, and their encampment quickly mushroomed into the city of Johannesburg.

It was quite natural for the deeply religious Boers to dislike these strangers intruding on land that they saw as exclusively their own. They called the incomers *Uitlanders,* foreigners, and despite taxing them, for the Uitlanders paid 80% of the Transvaal's tax, denied them a political voice. In a case of straightforward 'no taxation without representation,' the Uitlanders, whose gold was both creating much of the wealth of the republic and attracting the attention of Britain, resented this treatment. At a time when suffrage was an election issue in Britain, the Transvaal was an essentially undemocratic country. Not only the British but also any Catholic, Jew, woman or black African was denied the vote. Paul Kruger, president of the republic, appointed all the judges and controlled the government monopolies. Demonstrations and gatherings were banned and press censorship could result in newspapers being arbitrarily closed.

One of the many personalities thrown up by the Empire, Cecil Rhodes was then Prime Minister of the Cape Colony. He was a devoted imperialist who had secured a protectorate over Bechuanaland and had sent armed settlers to occupy that portion of Africa since known as Rhodesia, now Zambia and Zimbabwe. Rhodes dreamed of a world united under the Union flag, but for the present he wanted control of the 'hinterland' of the Cape, including the two Boer republics. One of Rhodes most loyal followers was the Edinburgh-born Dr Leander Starr Jameson, a veteran of the Matabele campaign who at this time was administrator for the South

African Company at Fort Salisbury, Rhodesia. In late December 1895, 'Dr Jim' led 500 troopers into the Transvaal, ostensibly to support the Uitlanders in a planned revolt against the Boers.

However, Dr Jim found that fighting the Boers was not the same as subduing the Matabele. He was ambushed and defeated at Krugersdorp, also known as Doornkop. While Jameson had sixteen killed among his 65 casualties, the Boers lost only one man, and humanely handed Jameson to the British, who sentenced him to fifteen months in jail. This episode, known as the Jameson Raid, resulted in Rhodes resigning his position. If the Boers were relieved to see him leave, they must have been dismayed at his replacement. Joseph Chamberlain, the British Colonial Secretary, appointed Sir Alfred Milner as High Commissioner for South Africa.

Alfred Milner was a professional politician and financier and in his own way as much an imperialist as Rhodes was. Along with Joseph Chamberlain and Paul Kruger, he has often been handed the joint responsibility of starting the Boer War. While Rhodes was fundamentally an individualist, Milner was emphatically a government man so where Rhodes acted in a cavalier, Elizabethan fashion, Milner utilised official channels. Although the Uitlanders provided the excuse for British anger, the reality was probably the gold mines. Paul Kruger was president of the South African Republic, a serious, dedicated man and also the puppet-master who pulled most of the republic's strings. The combination was tragically explosive.

When a Boer policeman killed a British man named Edgar, then walked free, over 20,000 Uitlanders sent a petition to the Queen in protest. Chamberlain advised that if the Boers were allowed to escape without censure 'British influence in South Africa would be severely shaken.' His despatch to Kruger recognised that Britain should not interfere with the affairs of the South African Republic, but also listed the abuses suffered by the Uitlanders. When Kruger's government responded by offering a number of seats in the Volksraad to Uitlanders, Milner requested more concessions. 'I am not ready to hand over my country to strangers,' Kruger responded, and began to arm the Boers. Milner reinforced the British army in South Africa.

From twelve thousand men, Milner wanted to build a force of fifty thousand. But Kruger did not intend to wait until the British army was so powerful. On October 9th 1899, he gave the British 48 hours to withdraw all their troops from the Transvaal frontier. When this did not happen, the South African Republic and the Orange Free State declared war on the British Empire. The Second Boer War, known to the Afrikaners as Tweede Vryheidsoorlog, the Second War of Independence, had begun.

It was October 12th 1899.

Chapter 2 : The Boers

These Boers who had the audacity to declare war on the largest empire the world had ever known were a unique people with a long history in Africa. It was on 6th April 1652 that Jan van Riebeeck arrived at Table Bay with orders to establish a staging base for Dutch vessels sailing from the Netherlands to the East Indies. The United Chartered East India Company employed him, and the colony he created slowly expanded into Africa. Within five years there were ex-Company men, both Dutch and German, farming inland, and they were shortly joined by free settlers and, in 1688, a couple of hundred French Huguenots. These peoples combined to create a vigorous people who gradually spread inland as generations of sons left their fathers' farms and carved out homes of their own in the spectacularly beautiful interior.

These farms were totally dissimilar to the smallholdings of the European peasants. With so much land there apparently for the taking, every Boer wanted two farms, each of around six thousand acres, and when, around 1690, the Company prohibited further European immigration, the Boers looked to the native tribesmen for labour. The Old Testament appeared to allow slavery and as they became completely self sufficient on their own farms, the Boers of the interior saw no need for further dealings with Cape Town. Cut off from the mainstream of Europeanised society, these Boers retained the original 17th century ideas with which they had left their homeland. Staunch Protestants, they read the Bible and lived according to the words of the Old Testament. They believed that they were the chosen people and their trekking took them closer to the Promised Land.

With each generation demanding their own farms, the Boers slowly expanded inland and northward but it was not until the late 18th century that they reached the vicinity of the Great Fish River and met the southward advancing Bantu peoples. Until the arrival of the Europeans, only the San, known to Europeans as Bushmen, and the related Khoikhoi, known as Hottentots, had occupied the southern tip of Africa. These people were nomadic hunter-gatherers, small in stature but perfectly adapted to their environment. They had been no major hindrance to Boer expansion. The meeting of Boer and Bantu created a further complication in South African history, and there began a long series of Border Wars. These were known as Kaffir Wars, from the Arabic word for non-believer, and there were to be many between people of European stock and the Bantu people. Some of these wars involved the British army and British settlers.

After British administration replaced the Dutch in 1806, there was more interference with the Boers of the interior, particularly in the matter of the black slaves of the Boers. In the mid 1830s Britain declared that their anti-slavery policies applied to all the peoples of Cape Colony, and the Boers had to release their slaves. The compensation the British offered was small, and could only be collected in London, but few Boers had ever travelled further than Cape Town and had little inclination to leave Africa. Rather than submit to what they saw as impossible demands, many decided to leave the colony and the phenomenon named the Great Trek occurred. Around ten thousand Boers loaded up their wagons and trekked into the interior of Africa.

This movement could be likened to the Exodus, as a deeply religious people headed into an unknown land to forge their own nation. Legendary leaders emerged to take the dissatisfied people from their oppressors to create a better life in the north. Louis Trigardt was the first, the foremost of the Voortrekkers. His party rolled the furthest north, but they settled in unhealthy country and most died of fever. Piet Retief had other difficulties. His party nearly mutinied in the terrible crossing of the Drakensberg, but the women held them together and the Boer wagons rumbled into Natal.

After initial disasters, the Boers defeated a massive Zulu impi at the Battle of Blood River. This battle not only decided that war, but also taught the Boers much about fighting the native tribes. Chaining their wagons together in a circular laager, the Boers sealed the gaps with hastily cut mimosa thorn bushes. The Zulus had charged with their customary incredible courage and the Boer musketry blasted them away. Never backward, the Boer women had also fought, loading the single shot muskets and chopping down any warriors that reached the wagons. Even the children helped, melting lead and making bullets for their fathers' muskets. It was an epic encounter that matched Bunker Hill or Bannockburn in helping to forge a nation. However, it was only one battle of many.

Hendrik Potgeiter and Sarel Cilliers faced tens of thousands of Matabele tribesmen at Vegkop and although the Boer muskets beat them off, the Matabele decamped with all the Boer cattle. It had been a ferocious battle, with Boer women loading the muskets for their men and Matabele advancing in waves behind their long shields while their assegais lunged at the trekkers. One ten-year-old child who fought alongside Cilliers was named Paul Kruger, later known to the Boers as 'Oom Paul', Uncle Paul. The number of leaders in such a relatively small group of people points to both the strength and the weakness of the Boer character. Their way of life had formed the Boers into an individualistic people; they were not prone to taking orders. Very seldom was a single personality able to take and hold power over the entire Afrikaner people. When they left the Cape Colony the Boers were already divided, a collection of individuals rather than a unit. If a Boer could see the smoke of their neighbour's farm, then he was too close. They were family orientated, and although the men appeared to dominate their politics, women were just as influential in the private, and often in public spheres.

When the Boers arrived in the High Veldt they appeared to enter an empty land, for the native Sotho tribes had already been displaced by a series of terrible wars. Early historians placed the blame on the rise of the Zulus, but later research suggests that many factors contributed toward this devastation. Warfare between the tribes north of the Tugela River, combined with a widespread drought after years of comparative plenty, forced people to leave their homes. The tribesmen of Southern Africa knew this period as the *Mfecane*, the 'time of troubles' or 'the crushing', for it saw the scattering of many coastal tribes to the interior and the complete annihilation of some. Charles Maclean, a pioneer in Natal in the 1820s, wrote of 'heaps of human skulls and bones blanching the plains.' At least one million people are thought to have died in this terrible period, and the resulting depopulation led the Boers into believing that the High Veldt had always been empty. The more prophetic Boers believed that God had emptied the land specifically for them.

There were two distinct Boer states established in the north, the Zuid-Afrikaansche Republik or South African Republic – that later became the Transvaal – and the Orange Free State, and after a few years these tiny nations were at war with each other. Perhaps if they had combined they might have been more successful. but the Boers, like the Scots, were seldom a united people. After much wrangling, both gained formal independence from Britain, the Republic in 1852 and the Free State in 1854. This freedom was short lived however, and on the 12th April 1877 Great Britain annexed the Zuid-Afrikaansche Republiek and the Union Flag was displayed in Church Square in Pretoria. Naturally the Boers protested, peacefully at first and then, in December 1880, with some violence. The four colours of the ZAR flag fluttered at Pardekraal, a republic was proclaimed and within a few days the First War of Independence started. The British fired the first shot, attacking a commando at Potchefstroom in the Transvaal. At that time the British were heavily engaged in Afghanistan and had few troops in the Republic so had to rush up reinforcements. Pier Joubert, commanding the Boers, countered this by basing his men at Lang's Nek. On the 28th January 1881, 450 of the redcoated 58th Foot advanced shoulder to shoulder against the Boer, and lost 150 men. The 58th had fought with great courage, but once again Boer musketry had proved effective. There was a further British defeat at Schuinshoogte at the beginning of February, and then on the 26th of the same month, Colley led 579 men up Majuba Hill. The Boers promptly climbed the slopes, supported by covering fire and threw the British off. The cry of 'remember Majuba!' was to be heard during the later war. The Gordon Highlanders were particularly badly hit, and General Colley was killed. The Boers lost two men.

On 6th March 1881 Sir Evelyn Wood signed an armistice with Joubert, and the Pretoria Convention was agreed later that year. The South African Republic, now officially named Transvaal, was independent, although subject to Queen Victoria, while a British Resident was based at Pretoria to supervise the natives. After winning the war with some ease, the Boers wanted more. Three years later the London Convention removed British suzerainty from both republics; the Burghers were free of any British influence and the Boers perhaps thought they could live in peace.

When gold was discovered in the Transvaal in 1886, the Boers feared massive British immigration and passed an Act that Uitlanders – foreigners – could only vote after fourteen years of naturalisation. Eventually tension between Uitlanders and Boers led to the Jameson Raid, and finally to the Second Boer War. In their own minds, the Boers believed that God had granted them their land. They had carved out their nations in bitter wars and now all they wanted was to be left in peace to farm and squabble among themselves. If some saw them as intruders in Africa, they were no more intruding than were the settlers in Kansas or California or Queensland. They had trekked inland to escape the encroaching British and if in turn they had pushed others out, well, that was the way of the world. The black tribesmen that they had encountered were also invaders, for they had travelled from the north, removing the original inhabitants, the Khoikhoi and San.

Those Boers from the more remote farms were incredibly hospitable, like the Highland Scots, and perhaps that was because they were so isolated. The famous hunter and frontiersman, F.C. Selous in his book *Travel & Adventure in South-East Africa* noted this aspect of their character. 'Wherever their confidence has not been abused...no people in the world can be more genuinely kind and hospitable to strangers than the South African Dutch, whether in the Transvaal, the Free State, or in Cape Colony.'

What social life they had was centred round their church, and every three months they had the *Nagmaal* – Holy Communion, from

Night Meal, the Last Supper- when they mounted their wagons and trundled off to the Church for an entire weekend. It must have been a fascinating sight, with the matched spans of black or red oxen and the elderly *takhare*- very shaggy-haired man - who had amazing skill with the long whip. Many of the men had long beards and hair that grew below their collars. The women wore long, ankle-length flounced dresses with a mass of petticoats, while their complexions were protected from the sun by *kappies* – deep poke bonnets. A pure complexion was important to the Boers and perhaps the danger of the sun was recognised. The young boys wore *halfmas* (half-mast) trousers to mid calf. Despite their apparent isolation, the Boer church was very similar to the equally Calvinistic Free Kirk of Scotland. Indeed, many Dutch Reformed ministers were trained in Scotland.

The country Boers were slow of speech, polite of manner and they respected their elders. They had rolled out of the High Veldt or the Bushveldt, from farms and tiny villages with names like Zwagershoek, Coetzeespos, Melkrivier, Tarentaalstraat and Vier-en-twintig-riviere that could be two or three days' journey apart by wagon. The Bushveldt was roughly the area to the left of a line from Warmbaths to Messina and then north of a similar line extending southwest to the Pilanesberg. This entire section of the Transvaal was heavily wooded and once a centre of big game hunting.

Among the farms there were a few traders, Jewish or German, with solidly built houses, but most of the Bushveldt Boers lived in *hartbeeshuisies* or something just a little bit better. While a hartebeest is an antelope, the *hartbeeshuisie* was the name given to the roughly constructed house of a newly married couple. The typical Bushveldt house was a simple rectangle of pole-and-daga walls with small windows. The more luxurious had three rooms, with a minuscule kitchen protruding from the back. One room would be a bedroom for the farmer and his wife, and frequently there would be a long ox horn built into the wall to dispense with the necessity of leaving the building at night to answer a call of nature. Mainly the flat roof would be thatched, although there were both corrugated iron and shingle roofs to be seen.

Perhaps fifty metres outside the house might be a pit latrine, or a guest would be told '*Wat makeer die wye wereld?*' – 'what's the matter with the wide world?' Like other frontiersmen, these Boers had their own culture. They were cattlemen first and foremost, expert shots and excellent trackers. Central to their culture was the wagon, and the wagon whip. The bamboo stock was between three and four metres in length, depending on the number of oxen that were yoked together; twelve or sixteen. The joints were neatly trimmed and covered with a sleeve made from the tail skin of an animal that had been soaked and then shrunk in position. Occasionally the hair was left on to provide decoration.

The actual whip was made in three parts; sweep, *agterslag* and *voorslag*. The sweep section was three to four metres long and made from either giraffe or ox-hide tapering from about two centimetres to one centimetre diameter, sometimes being plaited from up to six slim pieces. The *agterslag* was next; made from thin, tapering kudu hide between one and two metres long, and finally the *voorslag*. This was also of kudu hide, about six millimetres wide, again soaked and then nearly doubled in length and halved in diameter by tightly wrapping another piece of kudu hide round it.

With these whips the Boers could slice flesh, flick a fly from the ear of an ox or crack them to signal to herd boys half a mile distant.
The Boers used giraffe hide for *riems* - reins. The entire hide was cut into a long strip about three to five centimetres wide, then looped loosely over a handy tree branch. The bottom of the loop was held in a curved length of tree-branch, which in turn was tied to a rock. A pole was thrust through the hollow created by the curved branch, and the riem-maker walked round the hide until it was tight against the top branch. The pole was then jerked out and the stone spun down, then the pole was thrust into the hollow between the stone and the curved branch so the riems wound the opposite direction. At intervals fat was smeared on, and after three or more days of this work, the riems were soft, pliable and dry.

The drivers of the ox-team had a selection of shouts, hoots and whistles, plus a clear, yodelling yell. Unfortunately this skill has gone. There is probably nobody in the world that can *inspan*, drive or *outspan* with the skill of these nineteenth and early twentieth century farmers. If the drivers knew every one of his oxen by name and colour and character, then the ox also knew his name and his position in the span.

Not long after the close of the Boer War, there was a *boeredag* held in Dwaalboom in the Western Transvaal about twice a year. A *boeredag* was a 'farmer's day', something akin to a Highland Games, or just a country fair. There were horse races and foot races, shooting competitions and tug-o'war. The shooting, of course, was incredible. and if the hopeful competitor could not hit a half crown at fifty yards, there was no point in entering.

There were also other games such as *sweepstok,* which consisted of a line of boys holding hands and running, with the largest boy at one end and the smallest at the other. When the largest boy decided that they were moving fast enough, he would stop and haul in his neighbour. Each boy had to speed up progressively as the line thus altered direction, but the last and smallest boy in the line would probably have his body pulled faster than his legs could run. He would be fired off the end, to fall heavily on the hard ground.

The boys also played *kleilat,* which could be translated as clay-switch. The switches were flexible and about a yard long, and were used to fire balls of clay with amazing power, speed and accuracy. The result was painful. There was also leg wrestling and *vingertrek* – fingerpull - for the men. The opponents locked the middle fingers of their right hands together and attempted to break the grip of the other. No other touching was allowed, and the result was often broken arms, fingers or dislocated shoulders. As can be seen, these sports depended on bodily strength and some skill, with an element of sadism. Unlike in British culture, there was no compassion for the loser or the weak. The winner crowed about his victory and the loser was not allowed to forget his weakness.

15

At Dwaalboom, and doubtless elsewhere, the drinking was regulated. Every hour on the hour from ten in the morning, a bell was rung and all the men lined up for a tot of *mampoer*. This was home-distilled peach brandy, although orange or the wild maroela fruit was sometimes used, and it was potent. No other drinking was permitted.

The Boer standards of manners were different to that of the British. In such a vast country, with huge distances between the settled communities and with farms frequently isolated by hostile land and sometimes-hostile tribes, there was a need for companionship. When a man met his friends, both shook hands and raised their hat, while if there was any sort of gathering, the men shook hands with every other man and kissed every female with whom he could claim some family relationship. On meeting any stranger, a Boer would almost immediately thrust out his hand and state his name. If the stranger did not give his name, the Boer would say *'En wat vouer u die van, Meneer?'* – 'And what surname do you bear?' If the name was one that the inquirer recognised, he could then ask if the stranger was related to somebody else with the same name. It was a quick and direct method of getting to know people.

Boer morals were strict, and girls in particular were kept under supervision. There was an interesting Boer custom of *opsitkers*, or 'sit-up-candle.' When a young man came to call on his girlfriend, the girl's parents had supper and retired to bed. The courting couple was left alone with a candle. When the candle finished, it was time for the man to go home. As the girl provided the candle, she also chose the length; the more she was attracted to the man, the longer was the candle. Women then, had a measure of control right from the start of the relationship.

Out in the veldt there was no contraception. People married young and a wife bore children in her own bed, with perhaps the local midwife to help. Women were expected to marry, with any (unmarried) woman unmarried in her thirties considered a misfit. Again there is a strong element of cruelty here; men had to be strong, women had to be wives and mothers. What cannot be forgotten was the sheer determination of these women. They had come on the pioneer wagons, they had loaded the muskets of their men when the native tribes attacked, and they ran the farms when the men were out on commando. Of course, on farms where there were no sons, or even where there were, the daughters frequently helped out on the heavy tasks and became as skilled and as strong as any man.

There were some women, such as Mrs Otto Krantz and Helena Wagner who rode on commando against the British. Mrs Wagner survived five gruelling months in the veldt. Others formed the Amazon Corps in Pretoria, and engaged in spying operations against the British, with J. Naude disguising herself as a British officer. By the rules of war, the British could legally execute such spies, but tended instead to admire them and impose light prison sentences. In the latter stages of the 1899 – 1902 war, women often escaped to the veldt to form 'women's laagers.' On these semi-permanent settlements, women did all the work, herding cattle, tending the wagons and looking after the children.

Once married, the Boers tended to remain in that situation. The Afrikaans word for 'man' and 'husband' are interchangeable, as are 'woman' and 'wife.' So much so that a man could call his wife *vrou* – woman- or the diminutive, *vroutjie*. The marriage bond was close, possibly made that way by the hardship and loneliness of the life where companionship and interdependence was essential.

It was possible to call a Boer a liar and have him argue his point of view without animosity, but if a man stressed his argument by pointing a finger, a Boer might well say '*Moenie vir my vingerwys nie*' – 'Don't show me your finger,' and then both grab the finger and break it, or demand that the finger-waver back down.

If one mainstay of the Boer culture was his farm, the other was his religion. Many of their descendants had fled Europe because of religious persecution and in the crisp air of the veldt, isolated from the European mainstream, their religion became even more important. When the British artillery at Magersfontein proved largely ineffectual, Christiaan de Wet said 'I ascribe our comparative immunity to a higher power, which averted misfortune from us.' They were Protestant, but being Boer, even their religion was divided into many sects and sub-sects. In that they were not too dissimilar to the Calvinistic Scots. In the rural districts the minister, (the dominie) was often the sole educated person, and if his religion was stern and unbending, then this did not always hinder the average Boer from being a fun-loving and hospitable person.

It is said that as late as the 1940s, when a Boer spoke to the minister on the telephone, he still raised his hat out of respect.

However, there were extreme sects. The Jeruzalem Gangers was possibly the best known, but others were as strict. Some sects believe that men can kiss each other in greeting, but men cannot kiss women in public. Any display of sexuality outwith the marriage bed is considered impure. On a lighter note, it was impossible to smoke a cigarette, or pipe, in the presence of these extremists, for *in die here Jesus se dae mense het nie gerook nie*! 'In the Lord Jesus' day people did not smoke.'

By 1899 there had been generations of Boers who had known nothing but their own culture. Africa was their home with all its superstitions and dangers and attractions. In their own way their communities were as isolated as the tribesmen with whom they communicated, or even the Inuit of the Arctic, and many of their opinions were archaic and inaccurate. It follows that their attitudes and ideas were outdated, geared toward their isolated lifestyle and basically unfitted for any prolonged contact with a mass of people from the more politically developed west.

These bushveldt farmers lived a great deal of their lives outside, and as well as the weather and large wildlife, they had to cope with smaller life forms, the insects. Africa is home to countless millions of these, but probably the two most destructive are the locusts and the flies. The words *Die Sprinkane Kom*! – 'The locusts are coming' could make even the toughest Boers shake. These creatures ate all the crops and the grazing, so leading to the loss of all the domesticated livestock. The Boers frequently did nothing to combat this menace, for the Bible suggests that the Almighty sent them as a scourge to punish the ungodly. It would therefore have been blasphemous to fight against them.

Yet the flies ultimately carried the worse menace of disease. Anybody working outside perspired and this perspiration attracted flies, by the score or by the hundred. Even inside, insects were a menace, and in the more affluent areas of South Africa, the best houses were equipped with fly screens. These were like curtains of fine copper-wire that had holes of around 1.5 mm., and covered all the outside doors and windows, plus the verandas and porches. It is unlikely that many of the back veldt Boers had such luxuries; like the other native Africans, they just endured.

In the bitter second part of the war, when the open warfare had ended and the Boers had turned to the hit and run guerrilla warfare for which their commandos were ideal, the British responded by clearing the veldt of the farms. Militarily, this made sense, for each farm was both a recruitment centre and a supply depot for the commandos. Even when the British had captured individual Boers, *'handsuppers'* in the colloquial phrase, and returned them to their farm on parole, there was no guarantee that the man would remain out of the conflict. On the farms, the Boer could rest and recover from wounds and exhaustion, then return to renew the conflict, or help the hard fighting commandos, either out of loyalty or out of fear.

However, once the British had removed the inhabitants of the farms this could not happen. In the Orange Free State nearly all the farms and most of the tiny towns, the dorps, were cleared of their inhabitants. One of the towns that the British left untouched was named Bethlehem, and folklore mentions a farm whose front wall was decorated by the Masonic Square and compasses. The commander of the demolition squad refused to either burn or ruin the building. These, however, were isolated instances; mostly there was no mercy. If the farmhouse could be burned, it was; if not, then the British killed a score or more sheep and tossed the bodies inside the building. After this, the British removed the women and children to refugee camps, bitterly remembered as concentration camps. In part, the people were placed in these camps to protect them from predatory natives, but the death rate was appalling.

Despite their differences, there was little personal animosity between the British and Boer fighting men. Deneys Reitz says 'Amid all the cruelty of farm-burning and the hunting down of the civilian population, there was one redeeming feature, in that the English soldiers, both officers and men, were unfailingly humane.'

During the battle of Hart's Hill in the campaign to relieve Ladysmith there was a truce between British and Boers. After shaking hands and accepting the British tobacco, the Boers discussed the war with General Lyttleton. 'How long do you think the war will last?' asked the Boers, to which Lyttleton replied 'It's only just beginning. We don't care how long it goes on. Fighting is our business. We've nothing else to do. But it's rather rough on you.' Then it was back to business and the men who had shaken each other's hands tried their best to kill each other.

Many of the women did not enter the camps. There were 'women's laagers' in the veldt, places where the women had formed the traditional defensive formation of the Boer. As the war continued, both the women's laagers, and the women left in the isolated farms that the British had not burned, were at risk from the African tribesmen. This added to the worry for the bitter-enders, those Boers who refused to surrender and fought to the last. There were many of these. When the war ended there were still 21,000 fighting burghers in the field. However, many Boers joined the British. More than five thousand of these handsuppers helped the British, either as National Scouts or guides or transport drivers. De Wet, the guerrilla leader, must have been chagrined to hear that his brother Piet led the handsuppers in the Free State. Most were from the *bywoner* class, the landless labourer who had no property for which to fight.

After the war the Boers did not tamely become part of the British Empire. Rather than fighting with Mausers and commandos, they fought with words and ideas. There were film shows that showed only the worst side of the concentration camps, there were pictures of army-issue bully beef cans with foreign objects found inside. Although these were ordinary army issue, and were canned in the United States, the propagandists claimed that these objects were deliberately introduced to harm the inmates.

Propaganda such as this was ground into the Boer people until they firmly believed that the concentration camps were a deliberate attempt to destroy the Boer people. The Afrikaner rising of 1914 was one result, and the refusal of South Africa to join the Commonwealth another. Apartheid, with all its horrors, may have been a third.

Chapter 3 : The British Army

In 1899 Britain was at the peak of her jingoistic period, but despite Kipling's poetry that lauded the prowess of Tommy Atkins and his red-coated fellows, the army remained an unpopular career choice. Pay was low, barrack conditions poor and discipline tough, but there were compensations. The army could provide excitement and travel, and being a soldier was marginally better than being unemployed. All the British servicemen were volunteers, with the minimum short service period being only six years. There were around 250,000 regulars, backed by nearly 80,000 Reserves. This was a minuscule force when compared to Germany's 3,000.000 or the 4,000,000 of France and when colonial garrisons whittled down the numbers, only around 70,000 men were available to deal with the emergencies that could crop up anywhere in the Empire. Indeed, Queen Victoria's army was often regarded as little more than an Imperial police force.

The ordinary soldier came from the lowest ranks of society and, despite a pay rise in 1896, still received, after stoppages, less than a shilling a day. On average they were not tall. Life in the towns of Industrial Britain had diminished the stature of the working man so they were smaller and less fit than the redcoats who had marched with Wellington and Moore. In 1899 the minimum recruiting height was 5 foot 5 and a half inches, but in 1900 this was reduced to 5 foot 3 inches, the same height as Lord Roberts[1]. Although the men sent to South Africa officially had at least one year's service, photographs of the campaign reveal many very young faces.

The vast majority of officers originated from the upper echelons of society. They lived better and longer lives than the men did. In 1900 the life expectancy of a working class man was thirty years, half that of a gentleman. However, after 'Black Week' in December 1899 when Britain suffered three successive defeats, volunteer units were

---

[1] In the *Soldier* series, Haigie is only five foot three. As he was recruited long before the Boer War, the judge who sent him into the Army must have ordered that his diminutive status be disregarded!

formed in Britain, and the City of London Imperial Volunteers provided a contrast to the usual social structure of the army. Included in their ranks were barristers, architects, bankers and civil servants.

In 1899 the British soldiers were dressed in khaki, not the scarlet that the Boers had found such excellent targets in the earlier war, but the officers still sported glittering stars and shiny accoutrements. As the war dragged on, even the officers became drabber, discarding swords and revolvers for the more practical rifle. The Highland regiments still wore the kilt, but after initial casualties suggested that the Boers found the sporran an excellent target, khaki aprons were worn. The Highland dress was obscured by the equipment that the men carried; twin cartridge pouches across the chest, criss-crossed white webbing disguised by a mixture of brown paint and cow dung, a neatly rolled greatcoat, water bottle, rifle, haversack, one hundred extra rounds of ammunition and field dressings. By the time of Magersfontein, most claymores had been discarded, for they revealed the rank of the owner to eager Boer marksmen.

In the initial months, the infantrymen carried the Lee-Metford rifle, although the Lee–Enfield gradually became more common during the course of the war. Both had a ten round box magazine that had to be loaded one cartridge at a time. As Mausers had their cartridges in clips, reloading was faster and easier for the Boers. Experience of earlier colonial wars had shown that at long range, high velocity rifle bullets could pass straight through a human body without causing sufficient damage to stop the target. The British had countered this by using soft nosed, 'dum-dum' bullets that expanded and broke up inside the human body with horrendous results. In 1899 the Hague convention had banned these bullets but both sides seem to have used them, often unwittingly, in this conflict. For example, when the British under Lt-Col Le Gallais surprised De Wet's commando at Bathaville on November 6th 1900 the Boer rearguard fought with soft nosed bullets. The wounds inflicted were terrible and when the British went forward with the bayonet, the soldiers wanted to execute every Boer who had a dumdum bullet in his pocket. It was a dum-dum bullet that mortally wounded Le Gallais, one of the better British commanders.

The men were trained to move by numbers and while the regiment was the home of the infantryman, the smallest tactical unit was a section of 25 men. Rather than firing as individuals, the soldiers still used volley fire, usually at the order of an officer. During the battle of Spion Kop, and perhaps on other occasions during the Boer War, officers ordered infantrymen to cease fire when they attempted to shoot without orders.

Supporting the regulars and reserves was the 144,000 strong Militia. Militiamen had to train for three months with the regular army, followed by one month a year. Like the regulars, the men were largely unskilled, and in some units the officers trusted them so little that they refused permission for them to train with rifles and live ammunition. There were also the Volunteers. 230,000 strong; they were unpaid and from higher up in the social scale. Lastly was the Yeomanry. Mainly rural and middle class they numbered around 100,000. At five shillings a day, their pay was five times what the infantry regulars earned, and equalled that of the Colonials. Unfortunately for the working class, the Yeomanry recruiters showed a definite preference for middle class men who could ride and shoot. However, the Yeomanry performed as well as any regulars in South Africa, and caused many a regular officer to blanch at their ability to think for themselves. During the Boer War, many of the Volunteers and militia saw no action, but spent their time digging trenches, building and repairing blockhouses or guarding lines of communication many miles from the front. The British Army had vast numbers of men in Africa, but only a small proportion ever saw an angry Boer.

But in any war, it was the regular infantry that bore the brunt of the early fighting. The next chapter consists of the unedited Boer War journal of an ordinary infantryman, Robert Brown of Methil in Fife, a private of the Argyll and Sutherland Highlanders. The only change to the journal has been to break the script into paragraphs. The spelling, grammar and capitalisation have not been altered.

Chapter 4 : Diary Of Pt. R. Brown No 4538 I A&SH.

'I left Richmond Barracks on the morning of the 28th Oct with the Argyle and Sutherland Highlanders for Queenstown Harbour where after the usual ceremony of telling of messes and stowing away kits we embarked on the S.S. Orcana bound for the Seat of War in South Africa and sailed at 5PM the same night. We received an enthusiastic send off from the inhabitants. The town was beautifully illuminated with different coloured lights and all the Ships in the harbour.

The men at the forts assisted to give us a hearty see off. We had to make the best of it so we all got settled down to it. We arrived at Cape St Vincent harbour on the 2nd November the voyage being good so far. We got our quantity of coal and water here and received orders to proceed to Cape Town with all speed. We left St Vincent that night settling down once more for the remainder of the Voyage some passing the time playing the cards others draughts or anything to pass the time.[2] Twice a week we had a smoking concert also a boxing compitition. A very sad affair happened on board about the 8th November, the death of Colour Sgt Hope of H Coy (Newmonia) the funeral Service was held and the band played the land of the leal and the body was commited to the deep. We had a fine voyage for the remainder of our time on the water.

We landed on the 17th November after 21 days sail at Simons Town Table Bay at 11 AM. We then entrained at 2:30 PM for De

---

[2] SS *Orcana* sailed on 27 October 1899 (not 28th) and arrived at the Cape on 18 November. Breakfast was coffee and porridge. Dinner was watery soup. If meat was issued it was often so fatty that the troops threw it overboard. Tea was a pint of tea with half a pound of dry bread. With no 'wet' canteen, the 'dry' canteen or coffee shop was popular. At night the troop deck was so crowded with hammocks that it was impossible to move save by crawling, while the deck was covered with sleeping men. The days were monotonous, but men had light duties; they could read or watch the dolphins and whales in the sea.

Aar.[3] We got a harty send off from the natives at Cape Town. When nearing Victoria West an accident happened which dropped our spirits a bit for the time being one of our men fell off the train and was run over. The inhabitants belonging to Victoria west Burried him. Nothing more of interest happened. We arrived at De Aar at 5 AM on the 19 November and remained there to get our mules and Transport carts. After staying here for 7 days the order came for us to entrain for Orange River a welcome order for us we were beginning to think we were not going to see any fighting at all but we saw more than we expected.

We arrived at Orange River where we Camped till next day when we again took the train for Belmont. On the road up we saw the battlefield of Belmont[4] and the smell from it was sickening we also saw the spot where the Guards Adjuntant was burried along with a few more. As our train got into the Station we received a telegram to push on a bit further and join Lord Methuens Division[5] which was 9 miles further on. We went as far as the railway was repaired then got of and marched about 2 miles to our Camp on the right of the line. It was 10 PM and the night was very dark the road was very hard to find the first thing that we heard was Halt who goes there from the out posts then we passed 2 or 3 different piquets and got to our ground where we piled arms and lay down after we had a drink of tea. We had only our Great coats so we had to make the best of it. The night was bitter cold.

We got wakened suddenly next morning at 3 AM which was the 28th November the order was given out to parade at 4 AM, our batt. Acted as rear Guard. We had only got about 2 miles when we heard

---

[3] De Aar was the main railway junction of northern Cape Colony
[4] Belmont, Cape Colony. Scene of a minor victory of Methuen's over the Boers on 23 November 1899
[5] The Highland or 3rd Brigade was commanded by Major General Wauchope and comprised the Argylls, the 2nd Black Watch, 1st HLI and 2nd Seaforths. Methuen commanded the entire division.

rifle shots it was our Remington Scouts[6] that had got in touch with the enemy. We halted for a short time and changed our magazines and opened out to 5 paces interval. 1 half bat. In front being led by Col Goff and the other half being led by Major Wilson.

We commenced as being in the reserve the Guards being the fireing line. The order was then given to advance the bullets now commenced to patter in front and over our heads but we kept on steadily and before the battle was ten minutes old had got right into the fireing line. It was then that we got our baptism of fire.

To se the way we advanced you would have thought we were having a field day in Aldershot. The men were chatting away to one another as if nothing was going on. I think the first think that brought us to our sences was a Boer shell bursting over our heads. I can tell you it made us bob down for a minute. The Boers seemed to have the range for we were being picked off one by one it was pittyfull to hear the wounded crying for stretchers and water. We kept up a good fire but it seemed to take little effect as the enemy were strongly entrenched.[7] After lying there for about 6 hours with no water to drink and empty stomacs for we had nothing to eat from the day before I felt as if I could eat a boer never mind shoot him but there was no such luck as we had just to stick it as Tommy says.

---

[6] Rimington's Guides: a mounted body of 200 Uitlanders and colonials raised by Major Michael Rimington, a special service officer sent from Britain in July. Probably Methuen's most effective scouts, they became known as 'Rimington's Tigers' from the leopard skin puggarees that they wore on their slouch hats. In South Africa leopards were known as tigers. Because they were Uitlanders or colonials, they could speak Afrikaans and would have an understanding of the local African languages.

[7] Modder River; known to the Boers as The Battle of Twee Rivier. 28 November 1899. The Argylls were placed in the 9th Brigade under Major General Pole-Carew. At 6.30 they were in reserve, but within an hour they were part of the firing line. A British gun battery moved up to bombard the Boers but some of its shells landed among the British troops. Extending on both sides of the railway, the men on the right had little cover and were badly mauled.

It was a terrible sight to see these dead and wounded lying about. After lying there for two or three hours more we got the order to cross the line to try and flank them. We had to go over one at a time while the remainder kept up a fire. The enemy seemed to have the Railway marked off you would have thought it was raining bullets, it was a miracle how so meny of us got over safe.[8] We lay down on the other side of the railway and commenced fireing again for a while then we advanced again and did a nice flank movement but we suffered very heavily. We managed to turn the enemy's flank and I may say when we got down to the river I was thankfull my lips were parched and my tongue was swollen. I was glad to dip my head into the water regardless of the bullets that was flying about. I saw one of our fellows of ours getting shot through the head just as he was diping his head into the water but the enemy soon scattered when we got over the river. The artillery was shelling the position where we got across not knowing that we were there. One of our shells landed right into the middle of a section of about 20 killing two and wounding the remainder.

From the time we started untill the time we got over the river we had been engaged about 14 hours – we lost 131 killed and wounded – and I can say none of us were sorry when it was all over.

After the Boers retired we got formed upon the side of the river and camped there all night where we got a tot of rum and some biscuits. The next morning we were up at 5 AM 29 November and crossed the river again and remained all day. We had been starved for 2 days but we made up for it the next day we commandeered all the pigs and hens we could see. It was great fun to see the highlanders running after the pigs and hens with pig poles in their hands and I managed to get a hen I don't know how old it was but I should think it was a pritty old soldier however it went down

---

[8] It has been said that the Boers calculated the range by planting white markers at measured intervals along the railway line. Major Albrecht, once an NCO in the Prussian Army commanded the Free State Artillery. He dug the gun emplacements that both concealed and protected the Boer artillery.

beautifull I thought I had never tasted a sweeter bite in my life though it was only half boiled and so sault.

I was surprised to se how light hearted we all were after going through all the agonies of the day before but a soldier is well named as absent minded beggar we soon forgot our trouble in the afternoon we shifted about 1 mile and made our camp on the opposite side of the river. The next day my company was on outpost duty and I think they had forgot all about us for we were there for 25 hours and all that we got was 1 of these meat lozenges about the size of a farthing. We were told that it would keep us for another 30 hours I can tell you it was a bad lookout for us but we got relieved shortly afterwards. There were 3 of us sent away to get some water to a house where some scotch people were staying when we asked to get our bottles filled they told us to get out of the place. So much for our scotch friends those we were fighting for we had just to do about turn and go to a Dutchmans house we managed to get it there. I think we stayed on the first camping ground about 4 days then we shifted further on as the water was bad.

We got our tents up from De Aar and got them pitched we were about 5 miles from Magersfontein where the Boers had taken up position after they were driven from Modder River. We rested here for a while but we had some very bad weather the storms here were very frequent. The Boers tried to throw shells into our Camp from Magersfontein but they fell short our 4.7 inch guns belonging to the Naval Brigade was placed about 3 miles from where we were camped they did some very good work.

We lay here untill the 10 December Sunday when we got the order to parade at 3 PM we marched out of our Camp and went about 5 miles to our right front in a drenching rain. We then halted facing Magersfontein and our Artillery commenced shelling the hill untill it was dark we then lay down untill about 12 midnight when we got up and commenced our night march to attack the position.

The night was pitch dark and the thunder rolling a very good night for a night attack. Everything went in our favour untill we got within about 150 yards from the trenches we were beginning to think there was nobody on the hill at all we seemed to be so close to the hill that they were bound to know that we were there however we had not much longer to wait. There was a flash and report of a rifle and before we had time to realise what had happened it seemed as if hell had burst upon us you would have thought that the hill was in aflaim it was impossible to face such a storm of bullets. The whole brigade was thunderstruck. We first got the order to lay down and then we got the order to retire and open out so we had to retire to the back of a riseing.[9]

An officer of ours was running about with no helmet I think he must have gone mad for the time he ordered 12 of us to advance along with him but we had not gone 50 yards when we had to turn

---

[9] Magersfontein: Boer trenches were long and deep. They were well camouflaged with grass and acacia scrub. This battle saw the first use of Lyddite in war. The British thought that this new explosive would destroy the Boers. In fact, most of the British shells missed their target, but did warn the Boers that the British were coming. The third battalion in the advance, Wauchope had initially ordered the Argylls to the left of the Black Watch, but changed them to the right just before the Boers opened fire. While the leading companies joined the Black Watch in the firing line, the rear companies were to their right rear. Sergeant Hynch, Lt Nelson and a mixed party of Black Watch and Argylls disposed of 40 of the enemy, mainly Scandinavian mercenaries. In this battle Colonel Goff was killed and Major Robinson mortally wounded.

Wauchope carried his claymore, but it was Major Benson, later to command a mobile column, who carried the compass. A Mauser bullet killed Major Lord Winchester, possibly while he watched the belated launch of an observation balloon.

About half past one in the afternoon the Fricksburg Commando attempted to move to the flank of the Highlanders and Lt-Colonel Hughes-Hallet of the Seaforths ordered two companies to counter the attack. When these soldiers moved, the rest of the brigade followed, at first retiring slowly, then running as the Boers poured fire into them. The battle ended with the rout of the Highland Brigade.

back, bearing 6 dead and wounded behind us the officer being among them we formed a fireing line as best we could and advanced again but it was no use we were getting fired at from the right as well as the front. We advanced again and again but it was no use we had only to retireing leaving half of our men on the field. We next formed a fireing line to the right and attacked the enemy on the right of us we advanced untill we were about 500 yards from them then we lay down and started firing.

The 2 officers that were in charge of us were both shot one of ours named Young and the other was an officer commanding the Guards the Marquis of Winchester they stood up till they were both struck showing where to fire we had just to do the best we could after that. We crept up to them within about 300 yards then we charged. I could not explain what sort of feeling came over me I think it was a half mad sort of feeling but I know when we got up there I thought my time had come. I saw a Boer aiming at me as I thought about 3 yards away. I don't know how he missed me but I assure you I did not miss him. I managed to get him as he was turning to get out of the trench with my bayonet I shall never forget the look that was in that mans eyes as he turned. There was none of them escaped we took 7 prisoners the remainder were killed and wounded we then retired and the bugle sounded the Regimental call of each Regiment and assembly.

When the men fell in by Coy's it was then we found out how we had suffered the poor Black Watch returned with only 600 men out of 1100 and the Seaforths had 380 killed and wounded. My Regiment had 350 killed and wounded I was never able to get the proper number of killed and wounded of the HLI but I think about 300 more or less which shows how deadly the fire was. That was the 11th Dec after the roll was called we retired behind the guns and bivouced for the night with sad hearts. We got some biscuits and a tot of rum each that was all we had tasted from the Sunday it was heartbreaking with a reverse and no blankets or coats to cover us the night being bitter cold we were glad when morning came.

32

My Regiment was put on outpost duty the next day till the afternoon when we got the order to retire on Modder River again. Our Reg acting as rear guard we got back all right a few of the Boers were following us up but we put a volly into them which soon scattered them. After we got back to Camp we got the order to get ready for the funeral of the General Wauchope and the Officers and men that were brought back. I shall never forget that night we burried about 75 in one grave it would have softened the hearts of stone to se the way the men were torn up with the barbed wire some of them were fairly riddled with bullets some one was to blame for it.

Some of the men that was near Wachope when he was hit heard him say don't blame the men. The question was who to blame I think that question could be answered.

We remained at Modder River for some time after this but we were by no means idle we had to dig trenches all round for fear of a night attack being made on us. We dug trenches through the day and go on outpost duty at night. I was sorry for some of the men. Some of them had never been used to pick and shovel their hands were red flesh they did not let us get too fat on the meat they gave us.

It was here that we held Christmas and New Year and under the trying circumstances they passed off all right. We had sports which lasted for 4 days. Lord Methuen gave us the sports. The next thing was the march to Koodesberg we got the order on the 3rd Feb to roll our coats and perade at 5 PM we did not know where we were going.

The Brigade was formed up and marched off under General McDonald[10] at 7 AM. We reached Heagors Drift 8 miles along the river next day 4th Feb we marched 28 miles and reached Koodesberg it was a very trying march under a burning sun and no water some of

---

[10] Major-General Hector 'Fighting Mac' MacDonald. After Wauchope's death MacDonald reported to Roberts how the Highlanders hated Methuen for the slaughter his tactics had caused. MacDonald had risen from the ranks and was renowned for his bravery.

the men never reached there they were falling out and dyeing on the road side. We were marching along side of a river all the time but we were not allowed to go down for a drink it was a forced march[11] we had to be there within a certain time.

At 2PM we engaged the enemy and scattered them in all directions with the help of General French and his troops. 7 Feb we went back to Frazers Drift. 8th Feb we arrived at Modder River at 8 PM. It was then we heard that Lord Roberts was staying at the Hotel in Modder River. On the 10th Feb he gave the order for the men to fall in any dress he gave an adress to the Regiment saying we had done good work at Modder River we were the only Highland Regiment at the Battle but he said there is still a lot to be done and he ment to give the Highlanders a good share of it. He said he never went through a Campaigne without Highland Regiments and he did not mean to go through this one without them. He said little did I think when I inspected you at Dublin that I would have the unspeakable pleasure of having you under my command when he rode off the men gave him 3 hearty cheers and 1 extra for Lady Roberts.

On the 11 Feb we entrained for Englin. We arrived at 9 PM lay here all the night near the line. 12th Feb we envaded the Free State my Regiment was acting as rearguard. The Road was bad and our waggons were breaking down every now and then the watter also was very scarce here the sun was very hot too we were glad when we got into our camp at Ram Dam. On the 13th Feb we left Ram Dam and marched to Waterfall Drift. We commandeered a lot of sheep for dinner left that night again after we had an hour or two rest. On the 14 Feb we marched to Reit River. We all felt done up but we just had to stick it.

---

[11] Forced Marches: often while on forced marches across the veldt the troops were on half, or even quarter, rations. When there was no drinking water it was common for the men to put a stone in their mouth, the idea being that the stone helped to keep the mouth moist. It was frequently believed, perhaps with reason, that the Boers had poisoned wells with the carcasses of dead horses and cattle.

Five hours after we got in we had to be on the march again we had to shift at 5-30 that night. On 15 Feb we arrived at Clip Drift at 7 AM it was here that Cronge[12] was nearly captured by General French.

We left here at 2 PM and marched all night. 16 Feb we were on the march still half sleeping going along the road.

17 Feb. Still marching only halting for meals which did not take us long to swallow as it was very scarce. On the morning of the 18 Feb we arrived at Paardberg pretty well worn out. The Boers were shelling us when we went into Camp but we took no notice of it. We lay down for a few minutes but had to get up again on hearing the Scouts fireing.

The water had just been brought up for the breakfast but we were ordered to dress and fall in so we were doomed to again fight the Boers on an empty stomach. My Coy started off as escort for the Guns we did escort for them for a half an hour but we were ordered to join the fireing line. It was very hard to get up as we were the only Coy advancing at the time and all the fire was directed on to us from the enemy but we were very lucky we only got 20 knocked over while we were advancing both my right hand man and left hand man were knocked over while we were advancing I was just wondering when my turn would come but I was lucky enough to get up without a scratch. My right hand man belonged to Air Sgt John we hear the other was a Pte Turnbull belonging to Tunbridge in the South of England.[13]

---

[12] Cronge: short, popular and black bearded, he was also stubborn and ruthless. He had once been tried for torturing African natives. A hero of the 1881 war, he had also captured Jameson at Doornkop.

[13] Paardeberg: The Argylls were on the right of the brigade and merged with troops of the VI Division. Colonel Hannay, who had commanded the Argylls until June 1899 and who now led a body of mounted Infantry, was killed, as was Lt. Courtney of the Argyll's MI company. Colonel Hannay had been ordered by Kitchener to launch a right hook into the laager. With fifty Mounted Infantry, he charged to his death, two hundred yards from the

The battle was rageing now at full hight Shells and bullets flying in all directions. We could not se very well where the Boers were as it was very bushy we had just to fire into the bushes however we held our own all day the troops on the other side kept up a heavy fire but it did not seem to take much affect. They made a charge but they only got about 500 yards and had to lay down as they were getting over like rotten sheep.

It was in this Charge that Lt. Courtenay of the M.I. A and S.H. got killed. He was burried near the river. It was also in this battle that Col Hanny of our Regiment got killed he was commanding the M.I. before this. He was menchioned in dispaches 3 times it was him that tracked the enemy to Pardberg. The hunger commenced to get the better of the troops so we opened our emergancy rations as night wore on we went down to the River and got some water.

General McDonald was in command of the Highland Brigade at this fight and I may say there was not a braver man in South Africa he got wounded in the foot at the battle but refused to leave the field. This put me in mind of the Moddar battle the enemy stuck here all day but we had them surrounded so they could not get away. It was here that De Wet tried to get Cronge relieved but he had to retire on Poplar Grove. Our killed and wounded was 100 belonging to my Regiment and the Seaforths lost over 150 the Black (Watch) lost about 52 but I never was able to get a proper list of the whole lot.

We returned to Camp when it got dark but left an outpost to watch the enemy. We got some tea and a biscuit each but the hunger had wore of us by this time. As we lay down for the night some had a blanket others had none. On the 19 Feb we were up at first streak of dawn it was very dark we had to walk about to keep ourselves warm. We were just going to have breakfast when we got the order to shift

---

Boer lines. Again the Argylls found themselves face down in the veldt as they duelled with expert snipers who sheltered behind cover.
Paardeberg meant 'horsehill' but to the British it became 'Stinkfontein' from the name of a settlement close by. Cronje surrendered with 4,069 burghers, including 150 wounded and 50 women.

up closer to the Boer positions. We went about 1 ½ miles and camped on the right flank of the Boer Laager and my Coy was told off for look out to watch the movements of the enemy we remained there for about 3 hours untill the artillery came into action and took the range. About the 3rd or 4th shot that was fired the Boers put up the white flag to surrender so our Regiment was told off to go down to the river to take over the prisoners and the laager.

The whole Army was cheering and jumping about like madmen it was a happy moment for us but we were doomed to disappointment. We had only gone about 500 yards when the Boers started to fire at us it was a lucky think for we were stoped in time or else we should have all been cut up as we were in quarter Column[14] again. It had only been one of the many trichous tricks of Cronges to draw us on.

Lord Kitchener ordered us to retire behind the guns and every gun was trained on the enemy. They kept up a tremendous fire the 2nd shot that was fired after they showed the white flag blew up 1 of the ammunition waggons. The Boers got wild at this and they started shelling our hospital but a well directed shot from one of our naval guns soon silenced them.

It was a splendid sight to see the shells bursting above the lagger. I think there was 107 guns playing on them at a time where we were there was 2 batteries of Artilery and some naval guns. The snipers gave the naval gunners some trouble. 1 sniper a very good shot killed 1 of our naval gunners and wounded other 2 in thre shots at about 14 hundred yards.

After it got dark we retired back a short distance for the night untill next day 20 Feb. after breakfast we marched 300 yards from the enemy being a better position to watch them. It was on the 20 that the Boer relief came to try and get Cronge out of the trap he had led himself into but our Artilary shelled them out of it cutting them up terribly they were not long in retireing on Poplar Grove.

---

[14] Quarter Column: a very compact formation used for marching rather than for attack.

The Boer snipers still kept up fireing all day we were in danger of being knocked over every moment. Our Adjuntant was shot when he was giving out orders. On the 21st we went down to the river and got a bath the first we had got for about 14 days and we had to go 2 miles down the river for it. We were just as bad when we came back the 22nd Feb we went on outpost duty we were relieved at night and went back to camp. We could se everybody getting ready to shift soon after we paraded and marched about 2 ½ miles till we reached the main Hospital. We lay here all the night close to the river.

This was the first time I had the pleasure of seeing our officers shareing the same hardships as ourselves. We had just to lay down as we were with no blankets only our greatcoats and our helmets for a pillow. It was very wet all night and we had nothing to cover us. Some of the men had to be carried to Hospital next morning with the rheumatisms. On the 23rd Feb we crossed the river about 9-30 by means of pontoon boat carrying 20 men at a time before the Regiment got over. The cooks had our tea ready so we got what you would not call a breakfast then we marched 4 miles and formed up behind the naval guns and remained there untill the next morning when we got up at sunrise and marched off to a position where there were small trenches relieving the Cornwalls.

On outpost duty. We were just behind the Boer position scattered over a front of 1 mile. We remained here a while we used to watch the cattle coming up from the lagger and as soon as we got them they were killed and cooked before half an hour hunger drives a man to anything.

We were put on short rations owing to a convoy being captured.[15] We captured a few of the Boer pony's. I managed to get one and was sent down to the river to get some watter for the Coy but I don't think I shall ever forget that ride as long as I live. I was in the kilt as we had no trues with us I was not able to walk for 3 days after it. I

---

[15] De Wet's capture of a British column at Waterval Drift on 15 February caused serious supply problems for the British commanders.

don't think the poor brute had seen meat for a few days as its back was like a razor.

On the morning of the 27 Feb we heard volleys down near the laager it was dark and we could se the jets of fire. This was the Cornwalls who had got commision of the enemys position by the aid of the engeniers who had dug trenches through the night. About 8 AM 28th we had the pleasure of seing Cronge and about 4000 men surrender.

The troops now went mad with cheers, No 1 coy of each regiment went down with fixed bayonets in case of any treachery. We took good care we did not go down in quarter Column this time as we had had enough lessons. It was a fine sight to see 1 coy of each Reg advancing in fighting order from all directions it showed how completely they had been surrounded. Through the day so many of each regiment was allowed to go down to the laager.

The smell was something terrible I don't know how they stuck there so long but they had one advantage over us they could get fresh water and we had to take the watter after it had passed through their laager. Dead bodies and dead horses came down the river but there was nothing else for it.

The Prisoners were ragged looking mob they seemed to be very hungry for they devoured the biscuits we gave them like wild animals. They had plenty of supplies in the laager but they could not get near them our guns were all trained on them and whenever one of them showed their faces out of the trenches our guns put in a volley.

Cronge was escorted down to Moddar River by the Lancers. On the 2nd March we left Pardeburg and marched to a place called Voluchsantg just above the laager and stayed here intil 5th March. We then shifted to a place called Mahen's Drift we were on short rations since we left Ram Dam. On the 6th March we reached Poplar Grove by advancing along the river bank. I had the most responsible duty of being advance scout that day and I may say it was not the best of jobs however I got through it all safe.

The Boers had trenches dug from the river bed to the top of the bank but they did not stay there long. They were soon shifted when they seen the line advancing to attack them.[16] I was glad I was advance scout that day as it enabled me and my chum Pte Cassar belonging to East Houses to get a good feed. They had to run and leave their dinners on the fire. I think that was about the first meal I had tasted for about a month. I also got a Boer blanket out of the trenches which I brought home with me. I also got a bag of flour and a leg of meat.

I can assure you we enjoyed ourself at Mr John Boers expence that time you ought to have seen us making scones in our canteen lids. Of course we had no salt but it did not matter, beggars cannot be choosers so we had to do without.

We got served out here with boots to march into Bloomfentein.[17] We left here and marched to the place called Drumbool Camp 11 March. We marched from there to DryFontein where another battle

---

[16] Poplar Grove; 7 March 1900. The Boer trenches stretched for ten miles along a line of kopjes. Roberts intended to outflank the Boers with French's cavalry and mounted infantry, after which the artillery supported a three-division infantry attack. However as soon as the boers realised that the cavalry outflanked them, they retreated. Kruger led 6000 Boers in a run. French's cavalry did not pursue. Perhaps if he had, he could have captured both the Boer presidents and shortened the war. French and his Chief of Staff, Douglas Haig, blamed the failure on the poor condition of their horses, which they claimed was due to lack of fodder because of the raising of so many colonial units.

[17] Bloemfontein: with a population of around 4000, Bloemfontein was hardly an auspicious capital. The better houses were red brick with corrugated iron roofs, but there was a market square, a British insurance office and the Radzaal (parliament building) with ionic columns. Roberts captured the town on 13 March. The Press Corps and the Royal Engineers also claimed to be the first captors, and the troops renamed Bloemfontein 'Bobsfontein.'

was fought. We just came in at night as they were shelling the Boer positions. My Coy buried all the dead here. We Burried 104 Boers it was a terrible sight. I remember 1 fellow that we buried he was struck with a shell, all the right side was shot away. I have two of his letters, 1 was from his sweetheart, he had got it 2 days before he was killed. It said that she was dreaming about him being captured, little did she know he was killed. We also burried some of our own fellows, the Welch Regiment I remember 1 that we buried, he had his mothers letter in his hand. Another fellow, a Sergeant, he had his pipe in his hand[i]; he had been wounded in the head once and had taken out his pipe to get a smoke when he was struck in the head again.[18]

After we got them all burried we had to do the march to catch up to the Reg. We were just in time to get some meat and get down for a sleep.

The next morning we were up again as soon as daylight came in, marching to a place called Brandons Kop where we camped beside a railway. It was a sight to se a railway again. We had now some hope of getting full rations. It was here that we nearly caught a Boer train.

The lancers were in front of us, they charged but the driver uncoupled the engine and left the train, it was full of wounded. On the 14th March a train passed here for Bloomfontein. 15 March we left Brandons Kop at 6 AM for Bloomfontein, the town being occupied by General French. We bivouced on the left side of the town. The whole of the Highland Regs stayed here till we got the order to go to the relief of the MI at the waterworks who lost 11 guns.

We left on the 31st March. We left Bloomfontein and marched 23 miles to Bushmans Kop. We arrived 2-30 PM and advanced to the attack, we crossed the drift getting shelled by the captured guns. We

---

[18] Smoking: later in the war British soldiers often smoked dried cow dung

drove the enemy to the waterworks but had to retire on Bushmans Kop as the enemy was in great strength.

We stayed here until the 3rd April when we returned to Bloomfontein but left again on 4th April going 16 miles on reconnaissance. Nothing of interest occurred. We returned to Bloomfontein 6th April, the Brigade left again 24th April.

Mamema Camp. It was here I fell sick and had to go to hospital with dysentry[19] and enteric fever. I lay in the Highland Brigade Hospital for a while and then we transferred to the 8th General Hospital. The men were dyeing like sheep here on an average of 40 per day. You would often bid your bed chum goodnight and se him lying next morning sewn up in a blanket dead.

I got worse after I was transferred to 8th General. I knew nothing for 7 days but after that I got gradually better and was sent down to Cape Town. I must give the highest praise to the Colert people on the road down, they treated us splendid. Every station we stoped at you would find men and women waiting there night and day with refreshments. It showed how loyal they were to their Queen and after 4 days and nights in the trains we arrived at Cape Town and was then taken to a Hospital called Wyneberg.

I stayed there a few days to get my strength again a bit before going home. I embarked on the S.S. Biviavar and landed in Southampton on the 4th July after 24 days sail. I had to stay on the boat all night as we could not get a train to Shorncliff untill next morning.

We arrived at Sand Gate about 2 PM and was taken to a home close beside the beach. We could se the Cliffs of France on a clear day and we got very well treated. I stayed there till the 16th of July when I got my Sick furlough home. I can say I am fit and ready to go out and fight for my country again if required.'

---

[19] Dysentery – also known as 'the Modders' to the troops.

ENGAGEMENTS

Moddar River	28th Nov
Magersfontein	11 Dec
Koodesberg	4-5th Feb
Pardeberg	18 Feb
Poplar Grove	6th March
Dryfontein	11 March
Waterworks	14 April

No 4538 Pt R Brown I Bt A&SH

Chapter 5 : Horsemen And Border Reivers

Private Brown was a Fifer in a Highland regiment, but with the Scottish Borders still known as Scotland's horse country, it makes sense to make the hero horseman of the trilogy a Borderer.

For centuries, the borderland between Scotland and England was one of the most violent areas in Europe, if not the world. The narrow strip of land, only seventy miles from coast to coast and perhaps ninety miles from north to south, was the scene of some of the most bloody encounters between two of the most stubborn nations on earth. From Degastan to Flodden, Ancrum Moor to Otterburn, Carham to Hadden Rigg, Scots and English fought and died. By the Middle Ages, the nature of this borderland had led to the formation of laws, traditions and a way of life that was unique to the area. In November 1248 six knights from each nation drew up a code of thirteen articles that formed the basis of a code of laws that functioned only in the Borders. Added to throughout the centuries, this distinctive code operated until the accession of James VI to the united crown of both kingdoms in 1603.

Central to the Borders was a talent for survival and an independence of spirit that verged on the bloody-minded. On the night after the battle of Flodden in 1513, with the Scottish king and much of the Scottish nobility dead on the field, Scottish borderers plundered the dead while English borderers raided the supplies of their own army and, according to the Bishop of Durham, 'tooke diverse prisoners of ours, and delyveryd thaym to the Scottes.' Border loyalty was much greater than any sense of nationality, so it was no wonder that one Englishman reported that 'The borderours did full ill.' ('The borderers behaved very badly.')

By the fifteenth century, and probably long before, the horse was as important to the Borderers as it had been to the Mongol hordes or would be to the Boers. The Celtic peoples of Scotland had worshipped the horse, in whose guise the goddess Epona often visited this world, and as late as the seventeenth century some households placed the skull of a horse in the gable of their house to ward off evil. The Celts decorated their horses with face masks and harness discs, a practise whose echo persists in the brasswork and gleaming harness of horses at agricultural shows, even today. Pagan Celtic kings had to symbolically mate with a white mare before bathing in the broth of the slaughtered animal. Scotland's Celtic people held horse races in honour of their animal, and continued the ceremonies even after the advent of Christianity. On St Michael's Day in North Uist, young men and, sometimes, young women participated in bareback horse racing. It was in the Scottish Borders, however, that the culture of the horse reached its apogee.

Even today there is 'flapping' – unlicensed horse racing – in the Borders, and horse races are often included in the Common Ridings. These events are undoubtedly the highlight of the social calendar for every Border town, and are planned all year, video taped, discussed, treasured and jealously maintained. Developed from the ancient custom of an annual inspection of the 'marches', or boundaries, of the burgh to ensure that there has been no encroachment, the Common Ridings are a mixture of serious purpose, pagan festival and civic pride. Nowhere else in Britain is there such a display, and to witness hundreds of Border horsemen fording the Tweed in a curtain of spray, or thundering up a steep brae in the drizzle of a summer morning, is to witness living history.

Four of these Ridings are genuine, having continued without a break since the seventeenth century, or earlier. The burgh of Selkirk has the oldest, dating from the dour aftermath of Flodden. The Standard Bearer 'safe oot and safe in' can lead hundreds of horsemen from around the Border in a spectacle that has been termed the largest equestrian event in Europe. Hawick's events relate to the aftermath of the same battle, when the callants, the young men of the town, defeated an English force at Hornshole, capturing their flag in the process. Events include a mounted ceremony around the town, a blood-curdling gallop, horse racing and laying of wreaths at the war memorial. Each Border town has one of these, and it is sobering to count the names of the young men who left these sturdy towns to die for freedom.

The ceremonies of Lauder and Langholm are less old, but still predate the more modern ceremonies of other Border towns, all of which, however, are based around historical events or traditions. In every case save one, the main events are based on the horse. That exception is Innerleithen, a quiet town on the Tweed that stands aside from its proud neighbours. Such a xenophobic attitude is also part of the Border culture. The men of Hawick would say 'I'd rather be a lamp-post in Hawick than Provost of Galashiels', a feeling that is exactly reciprocated along the banks of the Gala Water. A visitor to the Borders may well feel an outsider, termed, for example, a 'stoorifoot' by the gutter bluids of Peebles, but there is nothing personal; centuries of surviving on the frontier has bred people more taciturn than usual for Scotland.

Fragments of the town wall of Peebles still survive, while castles, keeps and peel-towers crumble along the banks of every river and thrust skyward from hillside or solid farm. These are reminders of extreme violence, perhaps to be regarded as romantic now, but functional in their time and often containing ugly secrets. For centuries the people of the Border lived on the edge, ready at any time for the hammering hooves that signalled an attack, either by a full-scale army, or by the notorious Border Reivers.

In the 14th century the French chronicler and poet Jean Froissart noted that the Scots fought 'all a-horseback…the common people on little hackneys and geldings.' Along the Border these small horses were known as hobblers, and were surefooted among the bogland, forests and bleak, wind-scoured hills. The Kings of Scots imported breeding stock from Hungary, Spain and Poland and Scotland even exported horses to England. A law of 1214 ordained that every property-owning Scotsman must own a horse, and when Robert Bruce was at the height of his reign, Scotland could mount 20,000 cavalrymen from an estimated population of half a million. Nevertheless, while the Scots rode to war, they seemed to prefer to fight as infantry. Foot soldiers made up the mediaeval schiltron, the Highland charge and the feared mercenaries of the seventeenth century.

However, if the bulk of the Scottish Army did fight on foot, the Borderers were men apart. Officially known as 'light horsemen', they were the eyes and ears of the army, the scouts and skirmishers, intelligence gatherers and outriders. In times of war they would don their quilted jack, place a steel helmet on their head, take sword and, by the late sixteenth century, pistol, heft their lance and ride to war. Leslie, Bishop of Ross, said that the Borderers thought it 'a great disgrace for anyone to make a journey on foot.' A Borderer on horseback could ride anywhere that a footman could walk, and faster. He could fight with lance, sword or pistol, travel eighty, a hundred, perhaps a hundred and twenty miles in a long day, and spear fish from the rivers to sustain him. Deadly in attack, he was the master of the ambush, the night time foray; the vicious cut-and-thrust of the sudden skirmish, and could vanish into the hills in seconds. Overall, he was a good man to have on your side, but few trusted him.

Despite their many good qualities, the Borderer had a bad reputation. Whether mustered for his country or not, he was as likely to fight for his own ends rather than those of the king, and more likely to plunder than engage in a stubborn defence. When not fighting, the Border horsemen were renowned as reivers, night time raiders who could gather in small bands or armies of some thousands to raid their neighbours for cattle regardless of the national boundaries. Darkness was the reiver's friend, foul weather their ally, robbery and plunder their business, with murder common and cattle rustling their frequent aim.

The Border was tribal land, with family or clan names such as Armstrong and Graham, Scott and Charleton, Bell and Nixon, Maxwell and Hume. They could ride in a family group or join the outlaw bands of broken men. They could engage in bloody family feuds – the name originated in the Borders – engage in blackmail, which name was another Border invention, raid or kidnap.

Of necessity, the people of the Borders became more self reliant than most. Rather than depend on others to defend them, the victims of a raid could whistle up their neighbours and ride in a 'hot trod' to overtake the reivers. The Border Ballads are full of such incidents, while the earthier *The Fray of Suport* gives period details that remove any gloss of romance. Supposedly narrated by a widow, it describes a dour defence against attack:

> *'I set him to wear the fore-door wi' the speir, while I kept the back door wi' the lance;*
> *But they hae run him thro' the thick o' the thie, and broke his knee-pan*
> *And the mergh o' his shin bane has run down on his spur leather whang.'*

After gathering her friends, the widow exults

> *'Sae whether they be Elliots or Armstrangs*
> *Or rough riding Scotts, or rude Johnstones,*
> *Or whether they be frae the Tarras or Ewsdale,*
> *They maun turn and fight, or try the deeps of Liddel.'*

Not pretty words, but indicative of a fighting people. The Borderers, on both sides of the frontier, were not inclined to lie quietly under attack.

William Camden, the Elizabethan antiquary, wrote of these reivers riding 'in troops, through unfrequented by-ways, and many intricate windings...As soon as they have seized upon the booty, they...return home in the night...the more skilful any captain is to pass through those wild deserts, crooked turnings and deep precipices, in the thickest mists and darkness, his reputation is the greater.'

However, the Borderer's skills did not rest solely upon fighting and horsemanship. They could talk the devil out of hell. Here's Camden again. 'When being taken, they have so much persuasive eloquence, and so many smooth insinuating words…that if they do not move their judges…to have mercy, yet they incite them to admiration and compassion.'

Nowhere within fifty miles of the frontier was safe from them, and they dominated the region until that day in 1603 when the Wisest Fool in Christendom rode south to claim England's throne. The less organised Moss-troopers took their place, and the mayhem continued.

When not reiving or fighting, the Borderer expunged his restless energy with sport. Savage games of football were not unknown, but horseracing was more common. Some of the best-known names of the Border indulged their fancy, with the Earl of Bothwell attending a horse race in 1593 and the Bold Buccleuch organising the rescue of the imprisoned Kinmont Willie while pretending to enjoy the races. As well as the impromptu races that could take place virtually anywhere, there were official courses, at Langwathby Moor in northern Cumberland, for instance, and Kingsmoor by Carlisle. In peaceful days men raced for bells, such as the two preserved in Carlisle, but often the races were marred by undignified brawls. In one event at Strokstruther in Teviotdale in 1602 pistols were even drawn.

After the civil and religious wars of the seventeenth century, peace gradually settled on the Borders, and the farming skills that had always underpinned the economy came to the fore. The monks of the great abbeys had already created the border skill in sheep farming, while cattle raising had been part and parcel of work for centuries. In common with other parts of Scotland, grain was sown on ploughed fields, and the ploughman became an integral part of the landscape. The Agricultural Revolution changed the face of farming, clearing away the open plan run-rig farms as a hundred Enclosure Acts, from the seventeenth to the nineteenth centuries removed common land from the communities and increased the acreage owned by the gentry. Stone built farms spread, with thick walls, blue slate roofs against the frequent rain and fields frequently enclosed with dry stane dykes. Families who had once enjoyed a measure of freedom became servants of landlord and the clock, landless tenants who knew only work and the discipline of the Kirk. With modernisation, the horse replaced the ox as the chief labouring animal on the farm.

It was into this settled agricultural land that the society of the Horseman's Word spread, sometime in the late eighteenth century. The society seems to have originated in the North East of Scotland, and spread south, reaching even into East Anglia and Wales. Although the details were never entirely revealed, portions have leaked out over the centuries, to be mixed with myth and pure fabrication. There is no doubt that young farm servants were recruited in a bizarre initiation ceremony that included events of a quasi-mystical and occasionally semi-sexual nature. Perhaps because no women were allowed, initiates were stripped naked, although on some occasions they only had to bare their chests. There were a variety of stages in the ceremony, which included oaths of secrecy and ended with the initiate handing over a bottle of whisky to the Senior Horsemen.

The Horseman's Word society contained stallion walkers, farrier blacksmiths and farm horsemen. Its purpose was to teach the younger horsemen how to control horses through the magical Word, which in theory also made the Horseman irresistible to women. There is no way of knowing how old the society was; the rituals appear ancient, and may indeed have roots in pre-Christian times, but the society peaked in the nineteenth century. There are sources that insist the Word had roots in witchcraft, and cite the shaking the hand of 'Auld Clootie', or the devil as proof. True exponents of Wicca would distance themselves from any suggestion of devil worship, so perhaps Auld Clootie was intended to increase the fear factor for the youths involved. Secrecy was impressed on the youths, with various terrible penalties threatened if the apprentice Horsemen revealed any of the mysteries of the society. There is also a possibility that the original Horsemen were the inheritors of ancient knowledge of farming and horse-managing techniques that had been passed from generation to generation. With enclosures came more movement as families had to leave land that they had perhaps farmed for centuries. The Word may have been a vehicle for preserving craft, lore and fact.

In common with the original Masons, the Society of Horsemen was a trade guild, or a trade union, where the secrets of managing animals were passed on. It is possible that, lately denuded of most of their rights by enclosure, the Horsemen were attempting to maintain some status by adopting ritual and creating secrets that the gentry would never learn. Possibly women were excluded for the same reason; a desire to look important and retain the mystique.

Bearers of the Word seem to have been taught the skills of horsemanship. In their apprenticeship that might take two years, or as many as seven, they learned how to manage animals with soft words rather than by force, how to control working animals that were immensely more powerful and stronger than man. They learned how to cure illnesses and how to speak with the animals, how to make them relax. It seems that the Horsemen had significant words, such as 'two in one', which may have signified the union of man and horse.

In *Soldier of the Queen*, Drew Selkirk is initiated into the society of Horsemen, but it is only when he becomes appointed a lieutenant of irregular horse that he combines his Horseman skills with the arts of the Border Reivers. In South Africa he had a good theatre, for the Boer War was one where horses assumed an immense importance. There were many varieties of horse, from the cavalry chargers and Walers of the British Army to the Basutos, a mixture of oriental and thoroughbred animals that created a hardy strain suitable for local conditions. In a war where horses died by the thousand, a man with the skills of a Horseman would be in great demand, and his knowledge of horses invaluable.

Even today, the Borders region has a special affinity with horses, with more horses per head of population than any other part of Scotland. Augmenting the classic Common Ridings there is the annual Border Union show, which features horse shoeing, mediaeval jousting, horse jumping and heavy horse parades. Some of the guesthouses even provide stabling for their customer's horses; there are point-to-point races and national hunt races at Kelso Race Course. There are riding centres and riding schools, a three day horse trial event at Thirlestone Castle, endurance riding and the Buccleuch Country Ride. Connecting everything together is the annual Borders Festival of the Horse, which in 2004 attracted 1500 horses, with 2000 riders. Perhaps the Boer War was the last war in which British cavalry played a major part, but Andrew Selkirk and his Reivers would not feel entirely out of place in today's Scottish Borders.

Chapter 6 : The Course Of The War

After their declaration of war, Boer forces invaded both Natal and Cape Colony. In a matter of days they had driven the defending British forces into the town of Ladysmith, while in Cape Colony they besieged both Mafeking and Kimberley. Baden–Powell commanded the Mafeking garrison of less than eight hundred colonials, while at one time Piet Cronje had around seven thousand burghers, nine field guns and a 96-pounder Long Tom. Cronje's numbers, however, are disputed and certainly diminished to less than half that number. Cronje also had two 7-pound cannon that had been captured from Dr Jameson at the battle of Doornkop, but Baden-Powell, a master of improvisation, created one gun from a piece of steel pipe and a threshing machine and added another by repairing a 1770 vintage ship's cannon. He also used dynamite, thrown by Sergeant Page of Port Elizabeth, and three hundred armed Baralong tribesmen known as the Black Watch.

Beside Baden-Powell was Lady Sarah Wilson, aunt of Winston Churchill, who sent reports of the siege to the British press. To augment the shortage of supplies Baden-Powell, founder of the Scouting movement, stole food from the Baralong to feed the whites. When seven hundred Baralong women attempted to escape, the Boers caught many of them. Some were stripped and flogged before being returned to Mafeking.

During the siege one of the defenders would frequently creep out of the town at night, dig a shelter trench and conceal it with a green window blind. He would wait there until evening, when the sun was behind him and blinding the Boer. Then he would shoot any Boers he saw, with the Boers unable to locate him due to the sun's dying glare. When darkness fell, he quickly withdrew to the British lines. While Mafeking caught the public attention, the siege of Ladysmith in Natal was more important to the course of the war. Ladysmith was named after the wife of that earlier Boer fighter, Sir Harry Smith and it is perhaps fitting that this area should witness so much of the formal warfare.

The British Commander-in-chief was Sir Redvers Buller, a man of vast experience. He had fought in the Chinese War of 1860, the Red River Expedition in Canada in 1870, the Ashanti War of 1874, and the Kaffir War of 1878. Earlier South African service had seen him win the Victoria Cross fighting the Zulus. He was also involved in the campaigns in Egypt and the Sudan, and for all his subsequent defeats, the rank and file retained their affection for him. Although Buller has gained a reputation as a general who believed only in frontal assaults with the bayonet, he faced the brilliant defensive tactics of Botha and eventually he won. In the war of the creeping artillery barrages where the infantry advanced in short rushes from cover to cover and the step-by-step advances that relieved Ladysmith, Buller foresaw the shape of 20th century warfare. However, the British propaganda of the time favoured Roberts, and Buller was to be a maligned, misunderstood man.

De Wet perhaps understood the situation better 'whatever his own people have to say to his discredit, Sir Redvers Buller had to operate against stronger positions than any other English general in South Africa.'

Sending General Lord Methuen to relieve Kimberley, Buller led a force to Ladysmith. Methuen won his first costly action at Belmont on November the 23rd, followed this up by another at Graspan and then met de la Rey and the entrenched Boers in front of the Modder River. It was here that Private Brown and the Argylls were blooded, and although a flanking movement arguably turned the battle into a British victory, Methuen had lost 7% of his army. An even more costly 'Black Week' of defeats followed these costly victories. First General Gatacre tried a night attack at Stormberg. His men advanced in close formation and without scouts and were summarily defeated by a smaller Boer force. Seven hundred British soldiers were lost. Then Methuen ignored the advice of a colonial scout and a local tribesman and advanced his army straight at de la Ray's trenches at Magersfontein.

Colenso was the third British disaster, as Buller attempted to relieve Ladysmith. He threw the Royal Artillery and the Irish Brigade against the Boer rifles, with predictable results. Lieutenant Roberts, son of Lord Roberts was killed attempting to save the guns and even the Boer General Botha commented on the British attempts to save the guns 'Then came another lot, and another, and another…I was sick with horror that such bravery should be so useless. God, I turned away and could not look; and yet I had to look again. It was too wonderful.'

On the left flank of this battlefield, Hart sent his Irish Brigade forward in quarter column, marching for a ford in the Tugela River that did not exist. Caught in crossfire, the survivors lay down, unable to advance, unwilling to retreat, until Buller ordered them back. There were 1,100 British casualties.

Shortly after, Buller heliographed White, the commander of Ladysmith, and apparently advised him to surrender. When White refused, the siege continued.

Although Buller remained in the field, overall command was given to the 67 year old, one-eyed Lord Roberts, known to the troops as 'Bobs', who heard the news of his new appointment on the same day he heard of the death of his son. 'Bobs' was popular with the troops, and was remembered for his famous march from Kabul to Kandahar march during the Second Afghan War. He arrived in South Africa with the physically impressive Kitchener, whom he had brought as his Chief of Staff.

With Roberts and Kitchener in control, the tide began to turn. The army was reorganised, with units of mounted infantry raised to counter the mobility of the Boers. In February 1900, Roberts sent General French north on a march to Kimberley. Unlike Buller's offensives, this was a carefully planned operation that outflanked the Boer defences. French's cavalry defeated the Boers in a couple of skirmishes at the Riet and Modder Rivers, and relieved Kimberley on 15th February. Meanwhile Buller tried again for Ladysmith, losing 1,500 men in the terrible slaughter of Spion Kop.

With the loss of Kimberley, Cronje withdrew from his position at Magersfontein, but his slow moving column with its 400 wagons, its women and children, was harassed by the cavalry of French and then surrounded by hard marching British infantry. Proving that not only Buller could order fruitless attacks, Kitchener threw his infantry toward the Boer Mausers, and it was not until Roberts used his artillery that Cronje surrendered with around 4000 men. It was 27th February, the anniversary of the Boer victory of Majuba and the first major British victory of the war. The next day Buller finally relieved Ladysmith, but spurned the opportunity to pursue and capture the broken Boer army.

Now reinforced, Roberts ordered an invasion of the Boer republics. On the 13th March he captured Bloemfontein, capital of the Orange Free State and took Kroonstad on 12th May. Five days later Mafeking was finally relieved. For months Baden-Powell had defended this tiny town, and when the news of its relief reached Britain there was tremendous rejoicing. The word 'maffick' was introduced into the English language. Meanwhile, Buller was still plugging away in Natal. In May he defeated the Boers at Glencoe and Dundee, and then heading for the Transvaal.

With the Orange Free State apparently subdued, Roberts moved into the Transvaal, the South African Republic. On 31st May Johannesburg was captured, followed five days later by Pretoria. Within a month Roberts and Buller met at Vlakfontein. When General Hunter trapped Prinsloo's remaining Boer army against the Basutoland border, Prinsloo surrendered. President Kruger hurriedly left for Europe. The British had repulsed the Boer invasion had defeated the Boer armies, and by 1st September 1900 had occupied both their capital cities and all their major towns. Roberts returned to Britain, leaving Kitchener to do any remaining mopping up. The war seemed to have been won.

Unfortunately, the Boers did not agree. Never happier than when on a horse, they began a guerrilla campaign. The war dragged on until the end of May 1902, with the British using a combination of farm burning, blockhouses, and columns to round up the Boer commandos. It was now that the colonial horsemen came into their own, and now that the true horrors of the war, the concentration camps, were erected.

Chapter 7:

'The Bleak Cruelty Of An Apathetic Parliament'

In November 1900 Lord Kitchener had been landed with the task of finishing the war. Lord Roberts had won the conventional battles and returned to Britain, but the Boers switch to guerrilla tactics caught the British Army by surprise. Roberts had already initiated a policy of scorched earth, with the civilian population of the veldt cleared from their farms and removed to camps, and in March 1901 Kitchener increased the intensity of this operation. Kitchener was aware that every farmhouse on the veldt was a possible source of supplies and sustenance for the commandos. He also knew that there was no glory to be won in defeating a few thousand horsemen, while every month of war cost Britain another £2.5 million. By the end of the war, the scorched earth policy destroyed an estimated 30,000 Boer farmhouses and damaged or cleared forty townships. The inhabitants, mainly non-combatants, women and children, were removed, often by force. Many had no opportunity to gather those belongings that were most precious to them before being bundled into ox-carts or the railway and transported into camps.

Originally named refugee camps, for non-combatants could take refuge in them, in March 1901 the Liberal MPs C. Scott and John Ellis called them 'concentration camps' and the term became widespread. The name originated from the Cuban rebellion in the late 1890s, when the Spanish authorities herded the civilian population into 'reconcentration' camps. In return the Secretary for War, Sir John Brodrick, claimed that the civilian inmates were voluntary refugees, which was patently untrue in the majority of cases.

In part, the people were placed in these camps to protect them from predatory natives, but disease and malnutrition killed thousands. No war is pretty, and no method of waging war can be kind to the participants, but by clearing civilians from the land and herding them into camps, the British created a bitter animosity that still has repercussions. Although not intended as a punitive method against the civilians involved, the camps proved a killing ground for the Boer women and children. Used to a free life on their family farms, with space and independence, the Boer families had no idea of life in confinement. Often herded into overcrowded tents, they were fed army rations, with no meat allowed for those families whose men were still on commando. Vegetables were scarce and fresh milk for babies unknown, so the women lived on a diet of mealie meal, rice, potatoes, sugar and coffee. Children were rationed with tinned milk, meal, a small portion of meat and a miniscule portion of sugar and salt, with little or no vegetables.

There are many harrowing tales from these camps, but that of Lizzie van Zyl from the Bloenfontein camp will suffice. Emily Hobhouse related that she *"was a frail, weak little child in desperate need of good care.'* As Lizzie's father was one of the bitter enders, she was fed the minimum of food, so, according to Hobhouse, she became weak and ill. Only a month after her entry into the camp, Lizzie was sent to the new small hospital.

'Here she was treated harshly. The English disposed doctor and his nurses did not understand her language and, as she could not speak English, labelled her an idiot although she was mentally fit and normal.'

Disease hit the camp inmates quickly, spread rapidly and proved horribly fatal. Measles, typhoid, diphtheria, diarrhoea, whooping cough and dysentery stalked the lines of tents, despite all that the chronically few doctors and medical staff, with their limited supplies of equipment and supplies, could do. Out of an estimated Boer population of 200,000, 26,370 died in the concentration camps. Most, around 22,000, were under 16 years old. Four thousand were mature women. This figure compares to the nearly 22,000 British soldiers who died, of whom 13,250 died of disease. There were also over 7000 Boers killed in action. Similar concentration camps were created for black Africans.

As early as summer 1901, there had been disagreement on the efficiency of this veldt clearance policy. Some members of the military, and some Conservatives, thought it better to return the refugees to the countryside. Certain members of the military agreed, not on humanitarian grounds, but because the commandos would then have to care for their civilians, so making them less militarily efficient. Milner, not always accused of being overly humanitarian, stated in November that 'even if the war were to end tomorrow, it would not be possible to let people in the concentration camps go back home.' Milner however, had a somewhat ambiguous approach to Kitchener's methods. In June 1901 he stated that Kitchener's 'purely aggressive and destructive policy...may yet prove completely successful.' Yet in December 1901 and January 1902 he seemed to think Kitchener's policy was a 'blunder' and 'sad folly.' Kitchener announced his willingness to release the women and children as soon as the Boer leaders told him where to deliver them. While the politicians and generals wrangled, the people in and out of the camps continued to suffer.

With thousands of under-educated and uneducated women and children herded into these open camps, with poor latrine facilities and the presence of millions of flies, disease killed its thousands. There was no deliberate British policy of killing off the Boer population, nor was there any deliberate cruelty. If on the British side there was thoughtlessness, on the Boer side there was ignorance. As well as nearly non-existent hygiene, the Boer women treated the resultant fly-borne diseases with such homespun remedies as had been carried in the family since the seventeenth century, or had evolved from long use in the veldt. Deneys Reitz gives an example of this mentality in his book *Commando,* when a Russian society offered Piet Joubert a fully equipped ambulance and Joubert refused the gift. He explained to Reitz 'You see, my boy, we Boers don't hold with these new-fangled ideas; our herbal remedies are good enough.' However, such cures were more like mediaeval witchcraft than medicine, and what was effective in the open veldt, was terribly dangerous in a crowded camp.

Initially the camps had tents for shelter together with water and food for the inmates. Each should have been supplied with a camp doctor, with an interpreter if the doctor was not an Afrikaans speaker. There were blankets provided, and the accoutrements for a military camp kitchen. Unfortunately the camps had the identical latrine facilities as were used in the British army, but the inmates were not disciplined soldiers but backcountry farmers who were caught in a time warp of ignorance and medical superstition. Military organisation was not suitable for such people and it is noticeable that the death rate lessened when civilian authorities took over.

To the Boer children, and perhaps particularly to the women, living in such places was not only galling to their personal pride, but their national heritage. With no concept of hygiene in a crowd, they permitted the latrines to degenerate into a filthy quagmire that attracted flies by the million. The diseases were more aided than hampered by the Boer's own remedies. Frequently they refused the advice of the camp doctor. For instance, to cure a child of a fever and a cough, her mother might place a plaster of cow-dung on her chest. Not all camps were the same. In some there was cleanliness and co-operation, with so much fraternisation between the guards and the inmates that the former had to be changed frequently. Allegedly there was one occasion when there was so much good feeling at a camp and the guards that the Camp Commandant appealed for help to his superiors. The Commandant complained that the British soldiers and Boer women were physically fraternising. The resulting reply was not much help. 'Feed the troops on oysters and stout' it said, for both were reputed to help sexual prowess. However, that was an exception. Most of the camps were terrible places, full of diseased and bitter inmates.

At first unaware of the situation, the British public, and the world, were alerted by Miss Emily Hobhouse, who worked for the South African Women and Children's Distress Fund. She first visited the camps in the Orange Free State, and her fifteen-page report, *Brunt of War*, first sent to the Committee of the Distress Fund, but later published, led to outrage, horror and a desire to improve conditions. It was unfortunate that Milner did not like Hobhouse, who was regarded as a pro-Boer, so damaging any improvements to the camp system.

Emily Hobhouse was one of the few people who emerged from the Boer War with an enhanced reputation. Born in Cornwall in 1860, her grandfather was the Permanent Under Secretary at the Home Office and her father a parish minister. After a scanty education, Hobhouse looked after her widower father, while indulging in social work and following her interest in politics. After a trip to the United States, where she attempted to reduce the alcoholism among emigrant Cornish miners, she became engaged, but broke up and returned to England. Perhaps the hurt of her ruptured engagement embittered her toward men in general, but she was soon hard at work on the Women's Industrial Committee. In 1899 she became secretary of the women's branch of the South African Conciliation Committee, where she organised protests against the Boer War.

According to her own writings, it was 'late in the summer of 1900' that she learned of the 'hundreds of Boer women that became impoverished ...by our military operations.' With government permission, Hobhouse organised the South African Women and Children's Distress fund to help both Boer and Briton. Sailing to South Africa to organise the fund, ' in obedience to the feeling of unity...of womanhood', she arrived at Cape Town in late December 1900 and learned of the number of concentration camps. Family connections obtained a meeting with Lord Milner and permission to visit the camps with an interpreter and relief supplies, although Kitchener limited the number of places to which she had access.

Her first visit was to a camp outside Bloemfontein 'on the southern slope of a kopje right out on the bare brown veldt.' Of the 2000 inmates, nearly 900 were children. She wrote of the overcrowded bell tents, the heat, dust and rain. She mentioned the lack of soap, inadequate water and lack of fuel as well as the small rations. Most moving was the disease that seemed to have struck every family.

Hobhouse began a pressure campaign for soap and straw, more tents, kettles and clothes and above all, better medical assistance. Apportioning blame, she thought it was 'Crass male ignorance, helplessness and muddling,' and admitted, 'I rub...salt into the sore places in their mind...because it is good for them.'

Although her aggressive attitude would win her few friends among the establishment, with local people referring to her as 'that woman' and pointing out that her attacks were often ill-founded and biased, there is no doubt that her interference ultimately helped improve matters in the camps. She stressed the poverty of the sanitary arrangements and bad organisation, she spoke with genuine compassion of suffering families being transported from their farms to the camps, of hunger, thirst, disease and neglect, of hopelessness and suffering. 'I never had any doubt that every female countryman of mine would feel just as I did at the sight of all this' she wrote, and awoke the conscience of half the civilised world. Disappointed that her efforts achieved only partial success, her report on the ensuing debate in parliament was bitter. 'No barbarity in South Africa was as severe as the bleak cruelty of an apathetic parliament.'

Hobhouse toured the country, lecturing and speaking at meetings, often to be heckled by those who believed her to be pro-Boer. The press, with the exception of the *Manchester Guardian*, branded her anti-British and a traitor, friends cold-shouldered her and she was treated as a pariah, but she continued her crusade. Hobhouse raised considerable amounts of money in Britain and abroad and convinced the government to act.

It was in June 1901 that year that Sir Henry Campbell-Bannerman, the Liberal party leader, speaking from the front bench of the opposition, asked the question, 'When is a war not a war?' and replied to his own question, 'When it is carried on by methods of barbarism in South Africa.' Lloyd George, the future Prime Minister, also questioned the government, asking, 'Why pursue this disgraceful policy, why pursue war against women and children?' Other radicals and an Irish Nationalist joined the protest. Many in

Britain resented the implications and some of those who complained were dubbed as pro-Boers. Indeed, Brodrick claimed that the 'refugees' were 'contented and comfortable.' However, the conscience of others had been stirred, and the government acted.

Although grinding fine, the mills of justice are slow, and it was August 1901 before the Ladies Commission, led by Millicent Fawcett and without Hobhouse in its ranks, began its tour of inspection, and December before it completed its work. The Fawcett Report was equally damning of the camps, condemning the overuse of officialdom, lack of hygiene, lack of vegetables and slowness to respond to epidemics. Nevertheless, Fawcett also stated that it would be 'cruelty' to return the refugees to a veldt that was now largely denuded of shelter and food. Thankfully, the Fawcett Commission's recommendations were accepted, so the death rate in the camps dropped dramatically by February 1902 and continued to improve until it reached under two percent, around the same as any industrialised British city. However, by that time the damage had been done, with untold suffering among the civilians. There had been tens of thousands of deaths, including 12,000 black Africans, and a storm in justifiable international protest over the methods that Britain was employing to win the war.

As an example of international interest, the Foreign Office in December 1901 was handed a chart from a Swiss source, showing the annual children's death rate in British-run camps. The numbers rose from 160 per thousand in June to 433 per thousand in September. The corresponding figure in England was slightly over 60 per thousand.

By the end of 1901 military control of the camps ended and civilians took over. Kitchener also ordered his column commanders not to bring in any more civilians. Instead they were to remain on the veldt, where their farms had been burned, their crops destroyed and their livestock slaughtered. Militarily, this order also gave a greater burden to the Boer commandos, who not only had to fight the British Army, but also had to care for their own people.

After the Peace, Emily Hobhouse met the Boer generals who had fought so long. When they admitted that the suffering of their women and children had persuaded them to surrender, rather than the force of British arms, she expressed her admiration. The policies of Kitchener and Roberts had ultimately been successful, but if given the choice, it is unlikely that a majority of the British population would have chosen victory gained in such a manner. Trained to 'play the game' they might well have believed that to use such methods of barbarism was unfair, as well as uncivilised.

Chapter 8 :The Scottish Connection

Ever since the Union, Scotland has given generously of her manpower to preserve the freedom of Britain and never more so than during the 18th century. During the Jacobite rising of 1745, the clans had defeated regular soldiers in three pitched battles and had only lost a fourth when outnumbered and outgunned. Regular officers and English politicians advocated using the military qualities of the Highlanders for their own ends, with General Wolfe, who had already suggested genocide for Clan Macpherson, claiming that the Highlanders were: 'hardy, intrepid, accustomed to a rough country, and no great mischief if they fall. How can you better employ a secret enemy than by making his end conducive to the common good?'

William Pitt, Earl of Chatham and Prime Minister, followed the idea through, and for the next seventy years the Highlands were drained of men to fight in Britain's various wars. Some of these regiments, such as the 78th, Fraser's Highlanders, had a short, if distinguished history. Others, though amalgamated and altered, still grace the army. At the time of the Boer War, Scottish regiments had a very high profile. Prompted partly by the romances of Sir Walter Scott, partly by the love of Queen Victoria for all things Scottish and partly by their uncompromising tradition of courage, combined with the glamour of tartan and bagpipes, Scottish regiments were seen as among the best in the British Army. Incidents such as the 93rd Highlanders defence of Balaclava, immortalised as the 'thin red line', the relief of Lucknow and the Gordon Highlanders attack on the Dargai Heights had kept the Scots squarely in the public eye. There was little doubt in Britain that such infantry would have little trouble from the Boers.

In December 1900, Scottish regiments accounted for a substantial proportion of the British Army in South Africa. There was the Highland Brigade comprising the Argyll and Sutherland Highlanders, the Black Watch, Seaforth Highlanders and the Highland Light Infantry, as well as the Gordon Highlanders at

Ladysmith and the Scots Guards. Many more Scottish soldiers were to become involved in the weary months ahead.

When the Highland Brigade marched forward to relieve Kimberley, they were confident in their own ability. The Black Watch moved first, to lie in the mud while the British artillery pounded supposed Boer positions on the long ridge of Magersfontein. Some veterans suggested that the Boers might have dug trenches at the foot of the hills, but officers knew best and the artillery targeted the crest. In the small hours of the morning, 11th December 1899, the Highland Brigade led the advance toward the Boer positions. Marching in quarter column, with the men jammed close together, the brigade presented a splendid target for the Boer riflemen who sat tight in the trenches precisely where the veterans said they were, and which the artillery had ignored. With the British only a few hundred yards distant, the Boers opened fire.

Colour Sergeant McInnes of the Argylls remembered that 'the brigade seemed to stagger under the awful fire.' Other men spoke of the shock and horror, the confusion of contradictory orders and of men dropping like flies.

Most exposed to the enemy, the Black Watch gave way first, which started a mass retreat. Others remained on the veldt, returning the Boer fire as best they could as the sun gathered strength to roast them. There were heroes; Corporal Piper Jimmy McKay of the Argylls boldly stood up and played 'The Campbells are coming' while Mauser bullets thrummed around his head. Other pipers showed their regimental pride by similarly exposing themselves. Lieutenant Wilson of the Seaforth Highlanders actually led a company strength force in an advance that punched through the Boer lines, but was trapped by Boer fire. The survivors surrendered. The Highland Brigade lost heavily, with a quarter of the officers' casualties. The Black Watch lost 17 officers out of 22, and over a third of its men. As a military defeat, Magersfontein was bad, but worse was the knowledge that the Highlanders had panicked. It would take a lot to restore the battered pride of the Highland Brigade.

The Highlanders had lost all confidence in General Methuen and refused to fight for him again. It is possible that the brigade commander, Major-General 'Red Mick' Wauchope should have extended the men from their close formation earlier, but the Highlanders refused to blame one of their own. Morale was improved only when Brigadier Sir Hector MacDonald took charge. In February he led the Highland Brigade to Koodoosberg, 25 miles to the west, where they captured first a drift and then Koodoosberg Hill. It was a small victory, but restored some credibility. He was in charge when Kitchener again ordered the Highlanders to advance over open ground to attack the Boer laager at Paardeberg, with predictable results. However, this time there was no panic, and the Highlanders were able to savour ultimate victory when the laager surrendered.

At the beginning of March the Highland Brigade marched toward Bloemfontein, which was taken on the 15th and the following month they repulsed a Boer attack at Roodepoort, but that was their last major set piece battle of the war. However the individual regiments, together with other Scottish formations, fought until the final Boer surrender. The Black Watch cleared away the Boers at Susanna Fountain as the British marched northward, with the Seaforth Highlanders pushing the Boers from a ridge at Maqanstadt on May 24th 1900. Another smart action cleared the Bloemberg Ridge near Koorspruit to enable the brigade to reach Lindlay. By now the Highlanders had learned to use flanking attacks, decreasing casualties and unsettling the Boers. There were to be no more Magersfonteins, no more crippling losses, but the war had not yet ended.

Soon after the war started, the kilted regiments realised that the Boer riflemen were targeting their white sporrans that showed up so well against the dark tartan of the kilts. The Boers also liked to take the sporrans as trophies of war. By the time of Magersfontein, the

Highlanders wore khaki aprons that helped camouflage both kilt and sporran. It was another step away from the glamorous image of war and movement toward the drab professionalism that would be required in the 20th century.

Of all the Scottish Regiments, it was the Gordon Highlanders who had most cause to fight in the Boer War. They had taken most casualties in the affair at Majuba in 1881, and now they sought revenge, and the cry 'Majuba!' sounded in every sizeable action in which the Gordons took part in this war. The second battalion took part in the early victory at Elandslaagte, advancing with fixed bayonets against the Mausers. They also endured the siege of Ladysmith, with Colour Sergeant Taggart writing that he desired to 'get at the Boers and get the war finished.' Tragically, and typically, it was disease, not a Boer bullet, which killed the Colour Sergeant. It was the First Battalion that restored true pride to the Cocks of the North, fighting well at Hout Nek and even better when Ian Hamilton led them to victory at Doornkop where they advanced across burning grass to dislodge the Boers from a defensive position.

There were also Lowland Regiments involved, with the Cameronians performing good service during the relief of Ladysmith and becoming involved in the bitter fight on Spion Kop. The Cameronians held their position well, and when ordered to form the rearguard for a withdrawal, one infantryman was heard to ask 'what the hell are we leaving the bloody hill for?' Once again, senior officers had been found wanting and Scottish infantry had to pay the price. The Royal Scots, Pontius Pilate's Bodyguard and the oldest line regiment in the army, fought under General Gatacre, known to the troops as 'bach-acher', then spent the remainder of the war in long weary marches with only an occasional skirmish with the Boers. However, they were also involved in the siege of Wepener, where de Wet was repelled. The King's Own Scottish Borders shone at Elandsfontein in May 1901, when, together with the Derbyshire Regiment, they charged forward with the bayonet and recaptured a position that had been lost to the Boers.

As well as regular line infantry, Scotland provided cavalry, such as the Royal Scots Greys, who were particularly effective during the relief of Kimberley and the pursuit of Cronje to Paardeberg. The country supplied much of the manpower of the Scottish Horse, as well as the unique Lovat Scouts. Lord Lovat was given permission to raise this unit specifically for the South African War. Most of the Scouts were hill men from the Highlands, ghillies, stalkers and shepherds who were intended to out-stalk the Boer commandos. They proved effective as scouts, watching for the movement of the Boers with telescopes, and then reporting by semaphore and heliograph. In April 1900 the *Daily Express* lauded them, saying that 'the man who could outwit deer was not likely to overlook Boer traps.'

Overall, Scotland continued her tradition of providing men to fight for the Queen. If the Highlanders lost some of their lustre at Magersfontein, they won most of it back by sheer hard work and hard marching during the remainder of the war. However, of all the wars of Empire, the Boer War was the least favourable for infantry, for the horse ruled the veldt, and the Boers fought in a manner that British infantry found unconventional.

In 1902, the South African War was named the Great Boer War, but only twelve years later tens of thousands of Scots would again be fighting, this time in a war that spanned the world. From the trenches of France to Egypt, Scottish soldiers would again march forward with the bayonet, to add to their fame. The Germans referred to them as the 'ladies from Hell', but over 100,000 did not return. Some of the men of Mons and the Somme had fought at Magersfontein. Another 50,000 Scottish soldiers died in the Second World War, fighting for democracy against the twin evils of Nazi Germany and Imperial Japan. Scotland has always given generously of her manpower to help right the wrongs of a diseased world, but in both major conflicts of the 20th century, Afrikaans speaking men from South Africa fought alongside the Scots; history can show an ironic humour.

Chapter 9 : The Boer System Of Fighting

In 1899 the Transvaal regular army consisted of only 600 grey uniformed Staats Artillerie augmented by 1400 state police, the Zuid-Afrikaansche Republiek Politie, known colloquially as Zarps, while the Orange Free State had less than 400 artillerymen. In all the two republics possessed 75 pieces of Creusot and Krupp artillery. They also had twenty-three 37 millimetre Vickers-Maxim automatic quick-firing guns that could fire a belt of ten one-pound shells in two seconds. These were known as pom-poms and Conan Doyle, who heard them at Colenso, termed them 'the worst gun of all'. Except the artillerymen, all the Boer combatants were civilians, with less training than British yeomanry.

The Boers fought in loose bodies of men, usually with a local affiliation, known as commandos. A Commandant, who was elected by his district, led these. Each commando was divided into two or more field-cornetcies and each field cornetcy was divided again into corporalships. In theory each field cornetcy mustered between 150 and 200 men while a corporal commanded 25, but in such an irregular organisation these numbers were seldom adhered to. Although a burgher usually belonged to his regional commando, he was free to join whichever field cornetcy or corporalship he wished, so the more popular corporals or field cornets would have more men.

Although the Boers did not have uniforms, many of the commandants dressed in black coats and tall hats trimmed with crepe. The Boer republics did establish food depots for item such as coffee and sugar, but the commandos lived on mealie –maize - flour, or cattle that they either drove with them, or liberated while on the march. They could also find provisions at any of the farms of the veldt.

Apart from the artillery, the men were untrained save for an annual wappenschauw, a show of weapons, exactly the same name and function as in mediaeval Scotland, but the older men would train the younger in the tactics of the frontier. If they were outnumbered they

71

would ride up to the enemy and gall them with rifle fire, then withdraw, dismount, take cover and shoot away the enemies' advance. When the enemy got too close, the Boers would remount and ride away. It was a similar tactic to that used by the mounted bowmen of the steppes and had worked for the Boers for generations. Their last defeat had been at Boomplatz in 1848, when Sir Harry Smith had faced them with British regulars.

Their artillery was modern and the riflemen used a standardised German Mauser .276 with a five-bullet clip magazine and sights far superior to that used by British infantrymen. The evidence suggests that the Boers were superb marksmen, with an eye for cover unknown in the British army.

Although some back-veldt Boers were shaggy and bearded, many of the men came from prosperous farms or the little towns of the republics and would be moustached or clean-shaven. For a supposed nation of mounted horsemen, a surprising number were not horsed. These included the poor whites of the towns, and some of the *bywoners,* or farm labourers, of the veldt. While ordinary burghers frequently owned two horses, the wealthy possessed more and when the poorer burghers lost their sole animal, they were no longer considered a military asset.

On commando the Boer was as self-reliant as on his farm. He did not always accept discipline gladly and was inclined to argue. As the officers were elected, at least in the initial stages of the war, the entire military institution was too democratic to be efficient. After the initial stages of the war the commander in chief nominated the field cornets, people who had both political authority and social standing. The democratic Boer army had changed, and although efficiency was gained, perhaps some of the Boer way of life had been lost.

In the early stages of the war many burghers refused to leave the safety of the wagon laager for battle, but by the middle stage of the war this type of behaviour had largely stopped, possibly because many of the reluctant fighters had either surrendered or had returned home. As they were free agents, many burghers were able to choose when to go home and when to fight. This behaviour meant that numbers fluctuated greatly, which created a great problem for the Boer commanders, but it was a problem that lessened as the war wore on. Some Boer women were said to have sent their men back to war, for they thought higher of a fighting man than a shirker. When the war entered its final phase of farm burnings and concentration camps, this problem also ceased to exist. The fighting 'bitter-enders' frequently had no home to which to return.

The formations of the commandos also altered as the war progressed. In the first and second stages of the war the Boers travelled in great columns of wagons, complete with beds and stoves. When these were considered to be hampering the mobility of the commandos, they were abandoned. The Boer defeat at Paardeberg was partially attributed to their large number of wagons, and the fact that many burghers were reluctant to leave their possessions.

On commando the Boers constantly required scouts and sentries. Sentry duty was a nightly task, but in scouting the Boers excelled, with specialist scouting units, such as Theron's Scouting Corps, seemingly able to see everything that the British army was attempting. Danie Theron commanded an international brigade of eighty men and both his services and his bravery were a watchword among the fighting burghers.

Once the British had proved their masters in formal battle, the Boers reverted to a method of warfare that was far more natural to them, and suited both the size and terrain of their country. It was Oliver Cromwell who insisted that 'the best military weapon is a man on a horse' and the fighting Boers would certainly have agreed. From the exchange of massed musketry inherent in static battles, the Boers mounted their horses and began a guerrilla campaign that lasted for eighteen months and shook the British Empire, and was only quelled by tactics that bordered on the brutal.

One example of a Boer attack on a British camp, although on this occasion manned by Victorians was examined at the Court of Inquiry after the assault on Wilmanstrust, 12th June 1901.

'When the attack commenced the Boers advanced in a straight line through the camp discharging their rifles rapidly in many cases without raising them to their shoulders. The main attack came upon the front of the camp, but there was another attack at the same time, the fire from which swept across the rear of the horse lines at right angles to the frontal attack. This fire ceased directly the main line of the Boers reached the end of the horses, the latter continued to advance'

It was by swift, deadly assaults such as this that the commandos maintained their pressure on the British Army and unsettled the Empire. However, by this guerrilla stage of the war the Boers had difficulty in obtaining both clothing and ammunition, so procured supplies from the enemy. It was not unusual for Boers to wear the uniform of captured British soldiers, and many Boers used Lee-Metfords or Lee-Enfields and British ammunition. Apparently British soldiers were careless with their ammunition and a careful scouring of any British campsite would locate dropped or discarded cartridges. Unfortunately for the Boers, wearing the uniform of the enemy was against the rules of war and Kitchener issued a proclamation that any Boer wearing British uniform would be shot.

Many foreign mercenaries augmented the Boer forces. Germans, Dutch, Russians, Scandinavians, French and Irishmen joined the Boer forces. The Boer Irish Brigade blew up many railway bridges and culverts to delay the British advance into the Transvaal.

Even when the political leader, Paul Kruger, left the country, the Boers still had leaders such as de la Rey, de Wet and Louis Botha. Within months of the capture of Pretoria, their lightning raids had regained much of the initiative the Boers had lost. The British discovered that, although they controlled the major towns, the Boers dominated the countryside. It was de Wet who suggested the guerrilla campaign to the Boer higher command, and he matched de la Rey for skill and audacity. The commandos were to split into highly mobile columns that teased and taunted the ponderous British forces. In de Wet's commando, everybody helped with the menial tasks, so a laager could be mobile within ten minutes. But he had a short temper and if a man was caught sleeping on duty, he was sat on an ant heap, or flogged, which must have done wonders for morale.

Even as the British advanced, de Wet captured two hundred soldiers at Korn Spruit near the Modder River and followed that by capturing seven pieces of artillery and a further two hundred men. Not content with this, he led eight hundred fighting burghers to kill or capture six hundred Royal Irish Rifles near Reddersberg, and then swooped on the garrison of Wepener. Intriguingly, the garrison consisted of Afrikaners in British pay, and they defended themselves with some skill so that after a siege of sixteen days, de Wet withdrew.

The British began to realise that a new aspect of the war was beginning.

With only 800 men, de Wet captured another convoy near Heilbron '...two hundred bergschotten (Highlanders) with fifty six heavily laden wagons, fell into our hands.' A few days later he attacked Roodewal station. 486 prisoners were taken, 38 soldiers killed, 104 wounded. Hundreds of thousands of pounds worth of supplies and equipment was captured or destroyed. On the 31 May Piet de Wet captured the 13th Battalion of the Imperial Yeomanry, while on 11th July de la Rey captured nearly 200 men of the Scots Greys and the Lincolns at Zilikat's Nek.

In de Wet's own book *Three Years War* he claimed that he posted Brandwachten − watch-fire men while on commando. These men were the sentinels, and signalled to the bulk of the commando by means of fires. What worried the Boers most was not the possibility of British soldiers, but of Zulu attacks. 'We well knew what the

Zulus could do under cover of darkness...their name of "night-wolves" had been well earned.'

In March 1901, a commando led by de La Rey overcame a British force at Tweedbosch, and captured General Methuen. News of this caused Kitchener to take to his bed for thirty-six hours. Soon after he resorted to the callously efficient tactics that were to dominate the remainder of the war.

Initially the British attempted to catch the Boer commandos with cumbersome columns of infantry, but Kitchener eventually used a system of barbed wire fences, ditches and blockhouses to contain the Boers. In January 1901 these had begun life as a series of strongpoints to guard the vital railway but by May of next year there were over eight thousand blockhouses held by fifty thousand soldiers, and sixteen thousand native black Africans. Three thousand seven hundred miles of wire fencing sectioned off the veldt, with blockhouses placed every mile, or often less. Sweeps by British columns, supplemented by cavalry and mounted infantry scouts, drove the commandos against the line of blockhouses. Even if the Boers managed to penetrate the line, they had to fight the small garrisons, with inevitable losses. When it became obvious that the commandos were being fed and strengthened by the farms that dotted the veldt, Kitchener had the occupants removed to concentration camps. This led to much bitterness and many deaths as thousands of Boer civilians, unused to such conditions, sickened and died.

As the war dragged on, atrocity stories multiplied. While the Boers accused the British of deliberately starving the women and children in the camps, the British complained of Boers firing on British troops after displaying the white flag. The Boers also stripped British prisoners naked and left them to stumble home across the veldt. Wearing British uniforms, Boer commandos could approach close to British positions before attacking. Both sides also used the expanding dum-dum bullets that had been banned by international law, while Boers often agreed to stop fighting, only to return to the fray after enjoying a rest.

Atrocities and concentration camps changed the nature of the war. From being the last of the 'gentleman's wars' of the 19th century, the Boer War gave an ominous foretaste of the horrors of 20th century warfare. But Kitchener's policies were ultimately successful. In April 1902 he met the remaining Boer leaders and on May 31st 1902 a peace treaty was signed at Vereeniging. The news was greeted with relief and joy throughout the Empire. Kitchener's official telegram dated Pretoria, Saturday, May 31, 11:15 p.m., stated:

"A document containing terms of surrender was signed here this evening at half-past ten o'clock by all the Boer representatives, as well as by Lord Milner, the British High Commissioner in South Africa and myself."

In London, crowds gathered in the street, shouting 'Peace!' and singing 'God Save the King!" Around half had purchased small union flags, which they displayed with patriotic fervour. The Great Boer War had ended, and the Empire had triumphed.

Chapter 10 : Foreign Involvement

Although the Boer War was officially fought between the British Empire on one side and the Free Burghers of the two Boer Republics on the other, there were a number of outsiders who became involved, on both sides. Many nations hoped to see the pride of the British Empire humbled, and volunteers from overseas joined the Boer commandos. They came from Ireland, Italy, France, the United States, Austria, Germany, Russia, Norway, Sweden, Finland and Denmark as well as Belgium, France, Montenegro, Italy and Poland. Around five hundred of the foreign mercenaries were Dutch, and nearly eight hundred originated in Germany.

The Scandinavian contingent first met the British at the Battle of Magersfontein. Sheltering behind anthills and among the rocks, they joined their Boer compatriots in picking off the advancing Highlanders. However, when the Seaforth Highlanders closed, the Scandinavians tried to fight it out and were killed almost to a man. Seven out of fifty survived. They were buried in mass graves, which are today marked by white crosses. Their fate was typical of many of the foreign volunteers who fought beside the free burghers. However, they were only a small part of the international interest in the Boer War.

At a time when Europe was girding its loins and arming itself for a major war, conflict in South Africa also seemed inevitable. When the Boers adeptly snuffed out Dr Jameson's raid in 1895, the Kaiser's support was obvious. He sent a telegram to congratulate Kruger, and despatched a warship to Delagoa Bay. The British public became suddenly and temporarily anti-German. Perhaps they were unaware that many of the Boer farmers were descended from German settlers. The Kaiser was merely looking after his own distant cousins.

German public opinion was firmly on the side of the Boers, with stories of British atrocities widely published in Germany. One German politician, Herr Lieberman, speaking in the Reichstag, accused Chamberlain of being the 'most accursed scoundrel on God's earth' while calling British soldiers 'gangs of robbers and packs of thieves.' German academics joined politicians and press in vilifying Britain.

Nevertheless, the Germans were acutely aware of their own position in any impending South African struggle. In a memorandum by Baron Von Holstein of the German Foreign Office in June 1899, it is stated that 'We cannot possibly consent to mediate between England and the Transvaal...if we suggest to the Transvaal concessions which would make bad blood there, we should have unpleasantness with German public opinion. If we advise the British to cease their position as suzerain, we should face acute mistrust in our dealings with England...any decision not absolutely anti-British would be represented as partial and as the result of concessions made to us by England.' Despite the Baron's inability to differentiate between England and Great Britain, the message was clear. Germany wanted nothing to do with any future war in South Africa. The Germans, however, might have hoped that trouble in Africa would lead to worsening relationships between Britain and Russia.

On the last day of July 1899, Count Von Bulow mentioned the wider implications of a Boer war when he said that 'The possibility of a serious conflict in South Africa will make the British more compliant...when dealing with Russia. Even in the event of war in South Africa, the British Government would be very unwilling to...denude India, owing to the distrust of Russia so deeply rooted in England.'

Count Von Bulow put the supposed position of the major European powers quite clearly when he stated that Russia: 'has...declared that South Africa leaves it cold. That France by herself would stand up with the Transvaal against England is improbable, even though President Kruger might have received encouragement from Paris; he certainly possesses no binding and unambiguous promise in writing of armed support by France' and 'the British people would regard an appeal to European Powers, who are somewhat held in suspicion in

England, as a direct provocation.' In September, Count Von Bulow stated that 'it is ...desirable that the German Press should not fall into the errors committed by it during the Spanish-American war, in championing the weaker side...since France, Russia, Italy and Austria are not thinking of becoming enemies with England on account of South African questions, Germany cannot step forward and commit herself there all alone.'

It seems possible then, that each European power was waiting to see the reaction of its neighbours before making a decision. While nobody was willing to commit themselves to a war with Great Britain, each was hoping that somebody else might.

The Kaiser, grandson of Queen Victoria, later said that he had refused to join France and Russia in an anti-British coalition and had sent Queen Victoria his personal plan to end the early British problems. However, Lord Roberts did not need the Kaiser's help, nor the Prussian Order of the Black Eagle that the Kaiser insisted on bestowing on him. Despite the Kaiser's personal neutrality, however, during the war the Royal Navy stopped and searched German ships that were carrying war materials to the Boers.

The Boers, then, were apparently isolated even before the war began. However as soon as conflict seemed inevitable, the Boers searched for foreign help, but not for foreign involvement. Piet Joubert, the man who had won Majuba, wrote a long letter to Queen Victoria in 1899. He was hoping for a peaceful solution, but also sent copies to the Csar of Russia and the Kaiser of Germany, both men who headed powerful empires. Although ultimately it was Germany that would be Britain's enemy, in 1899 Russia was seen as the greater threat. The Great Game for domination of Central Asia had played a large part in British overseas politics for years, with Russia as the long taloned bear that threatened India. Twice in the past seventy years Britain had launched a full-scale invasion of Afghanistan to thwart perceived Russian threats to India, and Russia had also invaded that difficult Asian country. During the Crimean

War, Russian plans to invade India had been revealed, so Britain was always wary of the Csar's intentions in that direction.

Great Britain was also suspicious of the Franco-Russian Alliance of 1894. France and Britain had clashed over the Sudan as recently as November 1898, while Britain and Russia were rivals in China, Tibet and Persia. The state of the Ottoman Empire also created tension between Russia and Great Britain, which was always suspicious of Russians advances toward Constantinople and the Mediterranean. Although Russia never sent her army to aid the Boers, nor attempted to force the North West passes, Csar Nicholas was not personally neutral in the South African war. Stating that he was 'wholly preoccupied' with the war, the Csar told his sister that he read the British newspapers and 'could not conceal' his joy at 'yesterday's news that during General White's sally, two full British battalions and a mountain battery were captured by the Boers.' Jan Smuts, politically astute, hoped that the Russians might start another Indian Mutiny. Instead they sent a very efficient ambulance unit, as did the French, Germans and Dutch. However, Csar Nicholas's attempts to build an anti-British coalition between Russia, Germany and France failed. The Admiralty would be keenly aware that Russia had added to its fleet in the Black Sea and sent a squadron of cruisers to the Channel, while the Indian Army was monitoring reports that Russian army units had marched close to the borders of Afghanistan.

Speaking with his sister, Csar Alexander suggested that he should mobilise his troops in Turkestan to march on India. 'Not even the strongest fleet in the world can keep us from striking England at... her most vulnerable spot.' There would have been anxious men among the Guides at Jamrud, where the Khyber Pass hacks toward the Afghan hills, and the garrison at Peshawar would have been jittery, or perhaps keen at last to fight the old enemy of Crimea days.

There were undoubtedly many Russians serving with the Boer armies. Perhaps most were recruited from the ranks of the Jews who had fled the various pogroms in Russia and who worked in

Johannesburg and other South African cities. With Russia riddled with anti-Semitism, the burghers had to form two separate Russian commandos, one Jewish, one non-Jewish. The Russian Jews proved doughty fighters. Commandant Kaplan and Commandant Isaac Herman fought with distinction, while others, such as Josef Segal, nicknamed the 'Jackal' was an excellent scout who acted as secret agent for De Wet. Other Russian Jews, such as Benzion Aaron provided money for the Boer cause. No gentlemen when it came to war, the British deported captured Russian Jews to their homeland.

Despite the perceived threat of Russia, and whatever the Kaiser said, Germany was the European nation that perhaps had most input into the Boer War, both directly and indirectly. Men who had served in the German army trained the *Staatsartillerie*, the state's artillery of the republics. The gunners were well disciplined, wore uniforms in the German fashion and even marched like Prussians. The Boer riflemen also used the superb German Mauser rifle, with its excellent sights, killing range of 2,200 yards and five-cartridge clip that gave the Boers the edge in the early battles of the war.

Marthinius Steyn, President of the Orange Free State also hoped to use foreign influence to avert war. As well as contacting London, Steyn wrote to President William McKinley of the United States. McKinley, however, was morally unable, and probably unwilling, to help the Boers. The Americans had enjoyed British support in their recent war with Spain and were even then engaged in an ugly colonial war in the Philippines. However divided the American people might be on the subject of British Imperialism, the United States was fast creating its own Empire, while militarily it could probably do little against Great Britain anyway. Only Spanish ineptitude had enabled the United States to shine in the Spanish-American War. Individual Americans, nevertheless, were to contribute enormously to the war, on both sides. However, with many Americans comparing the British war against the free republics with their own war of independence in the eighteenth century, a large number of United States citizens hoped for a Boer victory.

Officially, McKinley removed his pro-Boer consul in Pretoria with the pro-British Albert Hay, a young man who was to look after British prisoners-of-war as well as British interests in the Transvaal. Another leading United States politician, Theodore Roosevelt, of Dutch ancestry with a smattering of Scottish blood, expressed sympathy for the Boers but in a letter to a friend, Cecil Rice, said 'it would be for the advantage of mankind to have English spoken south of the Zambesi, just as in New York.'

President Steyn, as well as Kruger, again contacted the United States, as well as France and Germany, when Roberts invaded the republics. He hoped for a negotiated peace, with the Boer republics remaining independent and those men from the Cape Colony who had joined the free burghers receiving a free pardon. Lord Salisbury penned the British response. 'Her Majesty's Government...are not prepared to assent to the independence either of the South African Republic or of the Orange Free State.' It was war to the finish.

During the early stages of the war, perhaps 2000 foreign mercenaries and volunteers shipped to South Africa to join the Boer armies. Confident in their own abilities, or perhaps suspicious of any foreign involvement, the Boers had not welcomed the international influx. 'Transvaal wants no foreign help,' Kruger had said, but graciously allowed the volunteers, many of whom had held high rank in European armies, to ride with the commandos. Many were brave soldiers, fighting and dying beside their burgher comrades, but their methods were more suited to European than South African warfare. As with the Scandinavians at Magersfontein, they remained in position when the British closed, only to be dispatched by vengeful British soldiers. According to Captain Carl Reichmann, an American military observer, the Europeans had more 'offensive spirit' than the Boers and often took heavy casualties in the assault.

One notable volunteer was Comte Georges Henri Villebois de Mareuil, a moustached and monacled veteran who had commanded the First Regiment of the French Foreign Legion. After Roberts' successes, he was appointed to command a new foreign legion on the veldt. 'Come and I will receive you here,' he wrote in a manifesto to Paris 'and ...we will show the world the mettle of which the French legionnaires are made.' As with the *Legion Estranger*, there were many nationalities, from the Hungarian Baron von Goldek to Count Pecci, a nephew of Pope Leo XIII. Some had fought in the Dutch East Indies, others in Indo-China or the Philippines, Cuba or South America.

There were even British deserters fighting for the Boers. One sergeant, a man named Greener, deserted to the Boers after being broken to the ranks for misconduct. Working alongside a cashiered English ex-lieutenant, he was captured and accused of showing the Boers how to dig proper trenches at the battle of the Modder River. The sergeants of his old mess burned his effigy in disgust. Another traitor, trooper E. J. Hays, was accused of helping the Boer artillery during the siege of Mafeking. The British put a reward of £50 on his head, but it seems he was captured during a raid on the town.

Portuguese came from across the border of Portuguese East Africa, Italians handled their stilettos, Americans vaunted their republicanism, but the local burgher population was not always pleased to see this international collection of roughs and adventurers let loose on the veldt. A good number were from the detritus of humanity, wanderers and the unemployable, who made up the numbers and terrorised the local burgher women,

On one occasion a party of fifty German soldiers, many of them officers, travelled across Portuguese East Africa to the Transvaal. Queen Victoria complained to her nephew, the Kaiser, who promptly denied that any serving German officer was fighting in the war. There was certainly a formed unit of Germans, perhaps 200 strong, many of whom died under the bayonets of the Gordons and the lances of the cavalry at Elandslaagte. A similar sized unit of Dutchmen was similarly treated. Many of the remaining foreign volunteers were killed or captured at Boshof on April 5th 1900, where Methuen's forces ambushed a party of around 70 French, Russians and Germans under Villebois de Mareuil. When de Mareuil was wounded, the volunteers hoisted a white flag but continued to fire until the British closed with the bayonet. Then they surrendered. Individual foreigners were also involved in more clandestine operations, with a German, Hans Cordua, accused of being the principal in a plot to capture Lord Roberts after his arrival in Pretoria.

In 1900 the Austro-Hungarian Empire was not the force it had been, but was still a major power that controlled much of central and Eastern Europe. Between one and two hundred men from this empire came to South Africa, with most of the officers from Austria and the ordinary soldiers from Hungary or the Balkans.

Cumillo Richiardi led a formidable Italian unit that had a reputation for ruthlessness, but it was the Irish and Irish Americans who perhaps made the most impact. Some had volunteered to help the Red Cross, only to join the fighting burghers as soon as they reached Africa. Others had been working in Africa, and most were filled with animosity over the perceived wrongs done by Britain to Ireland.

There were around 500 Irish and Irish Americans fighting on the Boer side during the war. Led by a man named John MacBride, whom the guerrilla leader Deneys Reitz thought 'brave but ugly' the Irish were initially ordered to guard the Boer artillery, the famed Long Tom guns that battered Ladysmith. They were prominent during the battle of Colenso, where men of Irish blood and Irish names shot the Irish regiments of the British Army, such as the famous Dublin Fusiliers, to shreds. They held the rearguard as Roberts pushed into the republics, but divided into two separate brigades in May 1900. The Irish-Boers were heartened by news that the Irish politician, Michael Davitt was speaking with the Boers in Pretoria, and that the nationalists Maud Gonne and Arthur Griffith were raising pro-Boer sentiments in Ireland and Britain. MacBride later married Maud Gonne, took part in the 1916 Easter Rising and was executed by the British. A brave man, his last words alluded to his time in Africa. 'I have looked down the muzzles of too many guns in the South African war to fear death and now please carry out your sentence.'

As well as MacBride, an American Irishman from Missouri named John Blake, who wore the dress of a cowboy and who had served as a lieutenant in the 6th United States Cavalry, led the Irish. Blake fought to the end of the war, although most of the Irish fled through Portuguese East Africa after the retreat to Koonisport. Among the many colourful Americans who joined Blake was J. Hassell, who had helped repel the Jamieson Raid. His American Scouts did much damage to the British. Some of the Americans adopted extravagant aliases, such as J.H. King, or 'Dynamite Dick' and James Foster the 'Arizona Kid.' To the British they were a nuisance, but never such a serious threat as de Wet or de la Rey.

However, some Irish-Americans decided to fight the war their own way. Rather than travel to South Africa, they took the war to the British Empire. Irish-American terrorists, operating under the name of Fenians, had already attempted invasions of Canada, and now they reasoned that Britain's difficulty in South Africa was their opportunity. Edward Bourke, an Irish-American said that the 'disasters to the British forces in South Africa should be a source of congratulation the world over' as 'the injury of England is of great moment to the Irish-born man.'

With many Americans wary that further Fenian attacks would weaken Canadian trade links or even push the United States into closer friendship with Great Britain, there was little enthusiasm for the campaign among those not of Irish blood. The British recruited the Scottish-founded Pinkerton Agency to check on the shipment of weapons from the United States to the Boers and observe any American recruits for the Boer armies. There was even a bizarre idea that Irish-Americans hoped to poison meat sent from Chicago to the British army.

More concrete was a plan by an ex-private of the American army named Magee to attack the Royal Navy at Esquimalt on Vancouver

Island. Recruiting a woman known only as Agent X, for the fee of $4 a day, the British struck back. Agent X was extremely efficient, inveigling herself into extreme Irish societies as well as joining the Wilhelmina Society, a Dutch association that was not averse to aiding the Boers. Irish societies of the time included Clann-na-Gael and the Knights of the Red Branch, but Agent X infiltrated them so effectively that the threats in British Columbia were snuffed out.

Irish Americans also attempted an attack on the Welland Canal in Ontario, dynamiting a lock gate but without doing serious damage. The *Daily Express* of April 1900 reported this attack as 'Canada Outrage…the fact that two of the three men arrested are Irish and the third a German – all Americans – supported the theory that the outrage was the work of Fenians or pro-Boers.' The paper then defused the political aspects of the situation by adding that the attack was 'a desperate plan on the part of certain American labourers…to prevent the use of the Welland Canal for diverting the grain traffic from Buffalo.' When the Canadian authorities tightened their security, the threats lessened.

As well as Irish-Americans, those of Dutch origin also tended to support the Boers, though not always by joining the commandos. The town of Holland, Michigan is only one example. With a population largely Dutch in blood and Boer in sympathies, it is hardly surprising that the local Republican party stated their support for the free burghers and a 'traditional hate of England' that apparently stretched back to the wars of the seventeenth century. Gerrit Diekema, the local congressman, pushed for the United States to recognise the republics and mediate a peace between them and Great Britain. Nearby Grand Rapids also had pro-Boer meetings, with collections of money, clothing and medicine to help the Boer cause, patriotic Dutch songs and many speeches. Much of the money was contributed by women and ostensibly intended for Boer women and children, and the churches across Illinois and Michigan also held collections for the Boer cause.

Nevertheless, there is no evidence that any citizen of Holland, Michigan ever travelled to Africa to fight, and once the tide of war turned, their sympathies began to wane. The volume of financial support dropped to a trickle as British victories helped the Dutch Americans realise that they were more American than Dutch. Other American pro-Boer organisations, notably the Lend a Hand Society of Boston and the Boer Relief Fund of New York, send food aid to the Boer prisoners of war in Bermuda. With the horror stories about the concentration camps shocking the world, some Americans even visited the prison camps at Bermuda. They seemed disappointed to find the Boers were well cared for.

In 1901 the British decided that subjects of the Queen who had joined the Boers, whatever their blood, should be executed. A number of Cape Rebels, men of burgher blood and speech who had been brought up under the British flag but joined the free commandos, were executed. Even some free burghers were shot, either for wearing captured British uniforms or for other offences. One such was Gideon Scheepers, born in the Eastern Transvaal, who led a commando through the Cape Colony despite all that the British Army could do. Captured after he fell ill, he was tried for murder, arson and maltreating natives. Found guilty, a squad of Coldstream Guards shot him on the 17th January 1902, much to the distaste of the soldiers involved, but his death brought protests from Germany, France, the United States and the Netherlands. Once again, however, indignation did not bring practical help for the struggling Boers.

Particularly in the early period of the war, when British forces suffered setbacks, European nations and others supported the Boers. With Britain the world's super power that had dominated global politics for the best part of a century, it was natural for other nations to see her torn down, her pride humbled and her armies defeated. However, deeds did not match the hopes and words. 'No people in the world', said Winston Churchill, speaking of the Boers to the House of Commons, 'received so much verbal sympathy and so little support.'

Even after Black Week, 10th to 17th December 1899, when the British military reeled under the triple disasters of Stormberg, Magersfontein and Colenso and defeat seemed a definite possibility, no foreign power sought to intervene. Bernhard von Bulow, the German secretary of state for foreign affairs, gloated that most 'German military experts' believed the end of the war would see 'a complete defeat of the English.' In common with many foreign commentators, he appears to have been ignorant of the Irish, Welsh, Scottish and Imperial involvement. In Britain, of course, national calamity created a new resolve, with the Queen Empress ending the complaints of one anxious politician with the splendid words ' Please understand that there is no one depressed in this house; we are not interested in the possibilities of defeat; they do not exist.'

After Black Week tens of thousands of British men volunteered to fight for Queen and country. The Boer War, which had until then been fought between a disinterested professional army and a nation fighting for its existence, had become a national war. It had also become an Imperial war as volunteers from Australia, Canada, New Zealand and other parts of the Empire rallied to the cause. The queen had been correct; after Black Week there was no possibility of British defeat.

Only when Lord Roberts had led the British recovery, the Boer republics had been occupied and the last large Boer army had been defeated, was it that the Boers actively sought foreign help. But by then it was too late. The Boers had resorted to commando raiding, hitting easy targets with a great deal of skill. Guerrilla tactics might cause the British temporary, if acute, embarrassment, but they would not win the war. All the Boer efforts to enlist foreign governments to their cause were fruitless. Dutch, German and American all spurned their hopeless advances. The Dutch, however showed moral support by naming the yellow and orange tulip 'General De Wet' in honour of the successful Boer general. It was a small prize for a long war.

In 1902 Britain responded to her obvious isolation by forming an alliance with Japan, whose press had been strongly pro-British during the war. Great Britain promised to support Japan if she should ever become involved in a war with two other powers, with a reciprocal agreement from the Japanese, who also improved their prospect of trade with the British Empire. Japan was then free to fight Russia in 1905, safe in the knowledge that no other power would interfere. With the death of Queen Victoria in 1902, King Edward, less inclined to friendship with Germany, initiated the 'entente cordiale' with France. The battle lines for the First World War were forming.

Chapter 11 : Help From The Colonies

Great Britain had traditionally used non-British forces to help defend and expand the Empire. In India particularly, Britain had used the available manpower to form military units that were later to prove the equal of any other force in the world. The Boer War was no different, except that it was the first war where sizeable contingents from the so-called 'white' colonies became involved in an overseas war. In this war, Britain did not draw on the splendid units from the Indian sub continent, ostensibly to retain the notion that this was a 'white man's war', but perhaps because the defence of India remained a high priority. With Russia always perceived as a threat beyond the North West Frontier, it would not have been wise to denude India of troops.

At first Britain had accepted help with some reluctance, specifying 'in view of the numbers already available, infantry most, cavalry least serviceable', and infantry from the colonies soon proved their worth. Sir Joseph Chamberlain, Secretary of State for Colonial Affairs, was well aware that Britain's rivals were hoping for British defeat in South Africa, particularly as many believed the war was not justified. He was also aware that Britain stood in splendid isolation, while Russia was manoeuvring for a possible alliance of powers against her. For these reasons, it was in the interests of the British Empire to give an appearance of strength and unity. As Chamberlain stated, 'by offering soldiers spontaneously and enthusiastically, the colonies would also demonstrate to a skeptical and hostile Europe the British Empire's reserve strength.'

Chamberlain need not have worried; the Empire rallied to the Queen. Canada, Australia, New Zealand and the colonies of Southern Africa offered men, Indian maharajas volunteered their warriors and horses, some of the Malay States attempted to send Malay States Guards, even newly annexed Lagos offered hundreds of Hausas. Before the end of the war, some 25000 men from Canada, New Zealand and Australia were to serve in South Africa, as well as thousands of South Africans. There were also small numbers of white colonists from Ceylon and India.

Until the Boer War, most of the colonies relied on Britain for defence, boasting only tiny defence forces and units of militia. Canada was no exception, where the city militia regiments provided a social function and supported the civil police power. The Canadian Militia, where necessary backed by British regulars, had proved adequate to control the occasional Fenian invasion and aid the North West Mounted Police in the west. The Boer war was the first occasion where Canadian units fought overseas, albeit under the overall command of the British Army. In a sense, service in South Africa helped develop the national feeling in Canada.

Sir Wilfred Laurier was premier of Canada, and knew that his country was split over the Boer War, with many French-Canadians arguing against imperialism while the British-Canadians believed the Empire was spreading civilisation. However, in October 1899 when the Colonial Office requested that Canada provide four units of 250 men each, he reluctantly agreed. As in Britain, there were spontaneous volunteers, with recruiting stations being able to pick and choose; so eager were the Canadians to fight. Eleven hundred men gathered at Quebec, under the official title of Second Battalion, Royal Canadian Regiment, commanded by Lieutenant-Colonel William Otter.

After two months training in South Africa, the Canadians showed their mettle at the Battle of Paardeberg, where they fought with fierce determination. With 18 killed and 63 wounded in their first day of action, the Canadians proved themselves equal to any of the British regiments involved, including the famous Highland Brigade. Paardeberg was the Canadians' first battle outside North America, and one of which they are rightly proud.

One of the Canadians, Sergeant James Kennedy, wrote of his experiences.

'We all fixed bayonets and charged, and such hell of bullets which greeted us when we jumped to our feet was appalling. I charged down to the bank of the river and observed that the surface of the water was being well rippled up with bullets.'

In common with the British regiments, the Canadian infantry could not advance further. 'As there seemed no possible way of crossing, and no sense in doing so, I turned and charged back to cover, making even faster time than on my advance.'

Canadians continued to play a full and growing part in the war. Their mounted units were amongst the best in Africa, while their artillery struggled through Rhodesia to join other Canadians who were among the flying column that rode to the relief of Mafeking. This journey was an epic. C Battery, Royal Canadian Artillery sailed from the Cape to Beira, then entrained in open carriages that jolted them across what was known as one of the worst railways in the world. Scorched by the sun during the day, burned by sparks from the engine, plagued by insects, they travelled by rail from Marandellas to Bulawayo, then to Ootsi. After leaving the railway there followed a 60-mile hike to join Colonel Plumer's army, and then they had to fight.

Colonel Otter's Canadians distinguished themselves when they cleared a series of kopjes near Sanna's Post when Ian Hamilton took a column to regain possession in April 1900. Watching British were impressed at the Canadians' use of cover as they advanced in short rushes, and despite Otter being wounded, captured the kopjes in a final rush. Canadians made such an impression on the opposition that one Boer woman is alleged to have told the Canadian artilleryman Lt. Morrison, that the Boers would only defeat the British when the Canadians returned home. Over 7,300 Canadians eventually fought in South Africa, losing 89 men in action and a further 130 to disease.

New Zealand was the first colony to offer military help. By the end of September 1899, when the war seemed inevitable the Premier, R.

J. Sneddon, backed by the New Zealand parliament, offered two hundred mounted infantry to Great Britain. Not yet aware of the high quality of these men, Britain nevertheless accepted. New Zealand had been responsible for her own defence since the end of the Maori Wars and had improved her Volunteer Force in 1893. By 1900 it was an efficient, khaki clad organisation with transport and medical units as well as horse, infantry and engineers. The South African War prompted a massive expansion of the force, which grew from 4,500 in 1898 to a peak of 17,057 in 1901.

Sneddon believed that Britain adopted a 'moderate and righteous' position toward the Transvaal and stated that the war was not truly with the Boers, but with 'all who are jealous of the growing power of the British Empire, and who, rejoicing in our reverses, are aiding and abetting the Boers.' Major Alfred Robin led 215 men to South Africa, where they arrived on 23 November. Posted to French's cavalry division, the New Zealanders first fought at Colesburg, where Christiaan De Wet repelled the British assault. The New Zealanders were more successful at Slingersfontein on 15th January 1900 when they repelled a Boer attempt to seize a height overlooking their camp. After the resounding victory, the name was changed to New Zealand Hill.

The New Zealanders arrived in ten separate contingents at irregular intervals throughout the war. The fourth contingent, raised and financed by the citizens of Dunedin, was known as the 'Rough Riders' after the United States horsemen who had fought in the Spanish War. All superb shots and horsemen, the fourth contingent, together with the fifth landed in Portuguese East Africa, where many fell victim to disease.

Most New Zealanders seemed to support the war, with the Maoris volunteering in some numbers. Despite the British desire for an all white war, New Zealand, decades ahead of most nations in race relations, accepted the Maoris into their forces. Indeed Sneddon encouraged Maori participation, stating that they were 'men as good as any Boers who ever pulled a trigger.' Maori chiefs agreed, with some 2000 men being offered.

By now combined into a single regiment, the first three contingents were involved in Robert's victorious procession to Johannesburg and Pretoria, but were unfortunate in the battle at Rhenoster Kop, where the Boer riflemen repelled a British attack.

By the middle of the war the British authorities had realised that horsemen were invaluable on the wide spaces of South Africa, and sensibly, if belatedly, requested horsemen from the colonies. Britain also paid the financial cost of recruiting these men. Although the intention was to use the New Zealanders of the fifth contingent to stiffen the British mounted infantry, they remained as a cohesive force. Most of the New Zealand contingents carried their own horses, making them an even more welcome addition to the British forces. However, one party of New Zealanders achieved a unique success when eleven dispatch riders riding bicycles near Hammanskraal, north of Pretoria, chased and captured ten Boer horsemen.

New Zealanders helped relieve Mafeking and Kimberley and faced defeat at Koornspruit, but were most notable in Kitchener's columns that hunted down the commandos. New Zealanders marched, counter-marched and skirmished with the Boers throughout the Western Transvaal, and scored a notable success on the 24 March 1901 when they captured General De La Rey's artillery and supplies, together with 135 prisoners. They also won a Victoria Cross, when Farrier Sergeant William Hardham ignored Boer riflemen to rescue a badly wounded soldier.

In common with other colonial forces, the New Zealanders served for a limited time, normally one year, with the first contingent returning home toward the end of 1900. The British troops had no such clause, and served in Africa for an unlimited period of time. However, with the war continuing and the Boer 'bitter enders' showing no signs of surrender, the New Zealand sixth contingent arrived to replace those who had served their time and returned to New Zealand. Landing in Africa in March 1901, the sixth operated in the northern Transvaal, with hard treks more common than hard fighting. Living in the open with poor food added to whatever they could forage, the sixth contingent were soon infested with lice. They showed the independent spirit of their nation by protesting with a 'ragged strike.' Despite such displays of individuality, the expertise of the New Zealanders was seldom questioned, with the *Times Hof the War in South Africa*, believing that experienced New Zealanders were 'on average the best mounted troops in South Africa.'

The seventh contingent proved adept at tracking the commandos and launching successful dawn attacks on their laagers. With Colonel R. Davies in command, the thousand strong Eighth Contingent arrived in March 1902, and the colonel impressed upon Kitchener that the New Zealanders preferred to fight as a unit, rather than have the men distributed among other formations. By the time the ninth and tenth contingents arrived in mid 1902, New Zealand had officially despatched 6,500 men to South Africa, and there were also individual New Zealanders fighting in other units. Of the 230 New Zealanders who died in South Africa, 71 were killed in action, 133 died of disease and the remainder from accidents.

Of all the colonies, Australia sent most fighting men overseas. At least 12000 men served in South Africa, with perhaps 4000 finishing their enlistment only to sign on a second time. Around one Australian man in fifty volunteered, and initially the war was popular, as the words of C. Clarke-Iron's music hall song, *Boys of the Southern Cross*, reveals:

We've heard about your trouble, Tom
In rousting out the Boer;
You shall not fight out there alone
Amid the cannon's roar,
The blood that stirred our noble sires
To build up England's Fame,
Re-kindles in Colonial sons

Their prestige to maintain.
For
We are the boys of the Southern Cross
Our stars shine on our flags-
Emblazoned with the Union Jack,
To show we're Empire lads. '

However, disillusionment set in when stories of farm burning and concentration camps reached home. The execution of serving soldiers such as Lieutenant 'Breaker' Morant also had an adverse effect on public opinion.

The British press took an active interest in the despatch of men from Australia, with the Daily Express on 24 April 1900 reporting 'Bushmen Embark…The Imperial Bushmen embarked to-day and were given a magnificent send-off…The New South Wales portion of the Imperial Bushmen, consisting of 750 officers and men, with 800 horses, embarked in the Armenia this afternoon.' The Express reported that Earl Beauchamp, Governor of the colony said 'an affectionate admiration was felt for them throughout the British Empire, from her Majesty the Queen down to the humblest boy in the streets of London.'

Each of the six Australian states sent separate contingents, with units from New South Wales and Victoria arriving in Africa as early as December 1899. Men continued to arrive until March 1901, with a final draft the following year, after the war had finished. Still at sea during the early British defeats, the Australians were involved in virtually every other campaign or engagement of the war. The Queensland Mounted Infantry and the New South Wales Lancers helped relieve Kimberley, where Cecil Rhodes and the Boer besiegers were giving Colonel Kekewich a hard time. The New South Wales Mounted Rifles were also present at Paardeberg, and the South Australian Mounted Infantry were first to enter Johannesburg after the New South Wales Mounted Rifles and the Queenslanders had fought a smart little action outside the city.

One action at the Elands River Post was most memorable. As part of the Rhodesian Field Force, commanded by Sir Frederick Carrington, 505 men were sent to defend a post at Elands River. Two hundred of the men were Rhodesian, the remainder Australians from Queensland, New South Wales, West Australia, Victoria and Tasmania. Commanded by Colonel Hore, a British officer, the force was soon surrounded by Jacobs de la Rey's commando of over 2500 Boers. After bombarding the defenders with artillery, de la Rey asked for them to surrender, offering an escort to the nearest British garrison. Colonel Hore refused, saying that his Australians would probably cut his throat if he were to agree. The siege continued, with the Australians sallying out by night to kill Boer sentries or damage their field guns. After a couple of abortive attempts, Kitchener eventually got through with a large column, but not before the defenders had eighty casualties, twenty of them fatal. Kitchener, never noted for his rhetoric, nevertheless expressed his admiration when he saw the position that had been held. 'Only colonials' he said 'could have held out and survived in such impossible conditions.' Conan Doyle gave even higher praise: 'When the ballad-makers of Australia seek a subject, let them turn to Elands River, for there was no finer fighting in the war.'

Nevertheless, to many Australians, the Boer War was characterised by long rides, bad food, poor conditions, the threat of disease and an occasional skirmish with the enemy. By the middle of 1901 there were few large Boer formations to fight, only an elusive, skilful enemy who had to be tracked and hunted like a wild animal. Much of the war was tedious hard work, but there was always the possibility of ambush, such as occurred to the 5th Victorian Mounted Rifles in June 1901. The Boers attacked in the late evening when the regiment was halted for the night at Wilmansrust in the central Transvaal. With the horses stampeded and the Boers dressed in British uniforms, the Victorians did not know at whom to fire and consequently were badly cut up. Nineteen men were killed, with 41 wounded, and the Boers captured the Victorians' pom-pom. The British commander of the column, Lieutenant Colonel Stuart Beatson, blamed the Victorians for not posting piquets and berated them as 'wasters and white-livered curs.' However, it was a British officer, Major Morris, who was later censured for his inadequately posted piquets.

Not surprisingly, the Victorians, all volunteers to fight Britain's wars, staged a minor mutiny. Like the Highlanders after Magersfontein, the Victorians refused to fight for Beatson again, with Trooper James Steele reported as saying it was 'better to be shot than to go out with a man who called them white-livered curs.' Steele and two others were arrested and sentenced to death, but Kitchener later reduced the sentence to imprisonment.

When the facts spread, there was anger in Australia, with Major McKnight of the Victorian Mounted Rifles demanding an apology or an explanation from Beatson. There was no apology forthcoming. Only when the Australian Prime Minister intervened in person were the three Victorians released from jail. This was not the only episode when Australians clashed with British authority. The case of Breaker Morant, executed for shooting Boer prisoners, is well known, but worth summarising. On 27th February 1902 a Cameron Highlander firing squad shot English born Lieutenant Harry Morant, known as 'breaker' for his skill in breaking in wild horses, and farrier sergeant Peter Handcock of the Second South Australian Mounted Rifles. Morant and Handcock, attached to the irregular Bushveldt Carbineers, had shot 12 Boer prisoners and a German that they believed had been spying for the Boers.

Morant did not deny shooting the prisoners but claimed that Lord Kitchener had given orders that all Boers who wore British uniforms were to be shot. There is some controversy whether Kitchener gave this order, as he seldom put things on paper, but much of Australia backed Morant, particularly when his Australian defence solicitor, Captain Thomas, a veteran of Elands River, cited other cases of atrocities, from both sides, and argued that superior officers had given the orders. There is also a possibility that Morant was retaliating against the torture and murder of his superior, Captain

Percy Hunt, who was captured alive at Duwielskloof but later found naked, tortured and dead. Neither side was innocent by 1902.

Much of the latter stage of the war showed the Australians only hardship, with much courage but little glory in the skirmishes with small parties of Boers. The New South Wales Mounted Rifles were reported to have ridden over 1800 miles between August and December 1901, with an average of three skirmishes a month. They had 24 casualties, inflicted 42 and captured 196 prisoners.

One method of investigating the impact of troops is to ascertain the opinion of the enemy. One man of de la Rey's commando wrote home after meeting the Australians at Eland's River. After noting that the Australians used 'our own tactics against us' he added 'they were the only troops who could scout our lines at night and kill our sentries while...capturing our scouts...Australians were more formidable opponents and far more dangerous than any other British troops.' Lord Roberts thought so highly of the colonials that he ensured that his personal bodyguard was entirely composed of them. Around six hundred Australians died, more than half from disease.

Nevertheless, there was more to the Australian contribution than fighting men. In common with the Canadians, New Zealanders and British, Australian also provided doctors and nurses, with the New South Wales Medical Corps being lauded as the best in South Africa. Led by Surgeon-major William Williams, the NSW Medical Corps operated a fleet of light, fast ambulances and efficient stretcher-bearers that first rose to prominence during the battle of Paardeberg. As willing to treat the Boers as the British, the Australians earned a bush-hat full of medals, including a Victoria Cross for Captain Howse, as well as praise, with Williams being promoted to Surgeon General.

Although India was not permitted to send fighting troops, she contributed a great deal to the British war effort. As well as the base for many of the prisoner-of-war camps, India provided supplies and a large number of medical staff.

Thousands of Indians travelled with British reinforcements who sailed from India. Although non-combatant, they served admirably as stretcher-bearers, doctors, veterinary surgeons, blacksmiths and bakers, grooms and transport drivers. In total around 10,000 Indians served in South Africa, but there was no official account of their work and no record of their casualties.

However, there was one 30–year old Indian lawyer who had organised an ambulance corps to help the British and while in Africa learned the art of passive resistance – saryagraha, or soul force of the Jain Hindus. One of the best known was the Natal Indian Ambulance Corps, mainly because its ranks contained Mahatma Gandhi, the later nationalist leader who sympathised with the Boers despite their attitude to the black Africans. 'My loyalty to the British rule drove me to participation with the British in that struggle,' Gandhi wrote in his autobiography. Working at Spion Kop, the Indians evacuated many wounded, including General Wingate, while at Colenso they carried Lieutenant Roberts. Both Buller and the local press praised their efforts.

Dressed in khaki uniform and slouch hat, these men did much to enhance Indian prestige, and proved their courage at the battle of Spion Kop where they helped the wounded under Boer fire. Despite becoming a sergeant-major in the Bambata Rebellion of 1906 Gandhi was to develop passive resistance to such an extent that he led his country to independence and began a movement toward independence that extended all over the Empire.

Overall, the contribution of the Empire was immense. From the hard riding horsemen to the Indian sweepers, tens of thousands of people from the Empire mustered to help the 'motherland.' As a display of loyalty from disparate nations spread all across the globe, it was surely unique, and reveals something of the success of the British Empire at that time. In a war characterised by bitterness and atrocity, Imperial unity was the one positive feature.

Chapter 12 : Horsemen Of The Veldt

Even before the end of 1899 it had become apparent that this was a war like no other. The British government had found that their infantry was lacking in field craft and ingenuity. Guerrilla leaders like de Wet could apparently strike at will and disappear into the dun immensity of the veldt. Using the maxim 'it takes a thief to catch a thief' the British government put out a call for people who could match the Boers at their own craft. Rather than infantry, the latest volunteers must be able to ride and shoot. There was an immediate response from the frontiersmen of the colonies: South Africa, New Zealand, Canada and Australia. Unlike most British infantry, the men from the colonies proved capable of matching the Boers in horsemanship, marksmanship and tracking ability. Indeed, the Boers were known to have asked Canadian prisoners to join them, as they shared so many characteristics.

Of the Canadian mounted units, among the most memorable were Lord Strathcona's Horse and the Canadian Scouts. In January 1900, Scottish born Donald Smith, by then Lord Strathcona and Mount Royal, suggested that he should raise, equip and pay for a regiment of horse to fight in the Boer War. Strathcona's Horse came into existence, comprising frontiersmen and cattlemen of the west, as well as members of the famous Mounties, all commanded by Sir Samuel Steele of the North West Mounted Police.

Arriving in Cape Town in April 1900, Lord Strathcona's Horse became scouts, tracking the Boers across the veldt and engaging them in murderous little skirmishes. When the Boers ambushed Strathcona's Horse at Wolver Spruit, Sergeant Arthur Richardson rescued a wounded man and was awarded the Victoria Cross. His actions reveal the bravery, as well as the skill and professionalism of the unit. Like so many mounted units, Strathcona's Horse was disbanded after the war, but was reformed in 1909. Today it remains a proud part of Canada's army.

Despite the Mounties' reputation of always getting their man, even Sam Steele's Strathcona Horse were unable to capture the elusive de Wet. However, rather than despair, they decided to honour their foe. Veterans of the Boer war held an annual Paardeberg banquet, where 'De Wet soup' was served. This delicacy included filthy river water, with 'corpse of horse' and 'graying gruel of mule.' The Canadian's unique brand of humour obviously helped them survive the harsh campaigns of the veldt.

The Canadian Scouts were another unit that carried Canada's name, although by the latter stages of the war, men from many parts of the Empire swelled the ranks. They were commanded and raised by the American born Major Arthur 'Gat' Howard, who had worked with the Canadian Militia during the North West troubles of 1885 and remained in Canada. Howard believed in taking the war to the Boers, attacking them as closely as possible. He personally raised the pay of his men, which must have added to his popularity. He also ensured that the Scouts had far more firepower than most mounted units by purchasing six Colt .30 calibre machine guns. However his bravery resulted in his death in action in February 1901. Charles Ross DSO succeeded him, one of the hundred or so Australians that fought with the Scouts. In common with many mounted units, there was also a troop of black South Africans who served as trackers and pathfinders.

The South African colonies had already sent many men to the front, with Rimington's Tigers perhaps the best-known formation. But there were many others. There were some Afrikaans-speaking riders with the British, in units such as the Cape Mounted Rifles and Brabant's Horse. De Wet called such people '...sweepings' and thought that '...they ought...to have been ashamed to fight against us.'

Natal itself, although arguably the least well represented of the South African colonies, provided over two thousand fighting men in such diverse units as the Natal Bridge Guards, Murray's Horse, the Colonial Horse and the Natal Naval Volunteers. One troop of the

103

Umvoti Mounted Rifles was predominantly Afrikaner and was promptly despatched to guard the Transkei frontier from any tribal incursion. Other Natal units, the Natal Carbineers, Natal Mounted Rifles and the Border Mounted Rifles, were amongst the first to challenge the Boers when they poured through the Tintwa, Van Reenen and Bezuidenhout passes on the 18th October 1899. There were over a thousand Natal men in Ladysmith during the siege and Lord Dundonald's column that relieved the town contained Natal Carbineers and Natal Mounted police.

When Mafeking was relieved, the first men to ride into the town were from the Imperial Light Horse, Uitlanders from Johannesburg with dust on their uniforms and ostrich plumes in their hats. The same men, led by Major Gough and 'Karri' Davies, had already relieved Ladysmith. The relief columns also contained the Kimberley Mounted Corps and one hundred men of the Royal Horse Artillery together with twenty-five infantry from each of the four nations of Britain. There were also veterans of the Jameson Raid. Other Colonials had no such direct reason to fight the Boers.

At this time many Australians were unhappy about relations with Britain. Although Australia was blessed with gold, vast expanses of land and a frontier mentality, much of her wealth was bleeding away to repay the interest on British capital investment. Ever since the tax on miners' licences in the 1850s had led to Eureka Stockade and the Southern Cross flag, there had been talk of a separate Australia. Now voices were raised to a shout of "Independence."

However, when news of British reverses at Magersfontein and Spion Kop reached Australia, the blood of relationship proved stronger than the water of politics. Volunteers came forward; firstly for the infantry that Britain requested and then, as the war became more fluid, for cavalry. Many of the British were dubious of the effectiveness of these Colonial formations. Douglas Haig named them 'Colonial Skallywag Corps' and thought that 'these ruffians' were 'good only for looting.'

Among the Australian Regiments were the Victorian Mounted Rifles, the Queensland Mounted Infantry, the New South Wales Mounted Rifles and the New South Wales Imperial Bushmen. Together with various British regiments, the Imperial Bushmen landed at Beira in Portuguese East Africa. Australian troops have always been more famed for their courage than their respect for authority. There is the story of Australian troops in the Korean War who picked up a British RSM in his full regimentals and threw him in a river. There is also the story of Brigadier Sir Bernard Fergusson who inspected a force of Australians while sporting a monocle. Next day every Australian paraded with the cap of a beer bottle in the same eye. A veteran of the Chindit campaigns in Burma, Sir Bernard plucked out his monocle, tossed it into the air and caught it with his eye. 'Now you do that' he invited. Such actions gained the respect of the Australians.

Possibly the respective pay scales helped create some of the animosity that existed between British and Australians. Where the British infantrymen were paid one shilling a day, the Australians earned five shillings. There is an echo of the bitterness that this caused in Kipling's *M.I. (Mounted Infantry of the Line)*

'When you want men to be Mausered at one and a penny a day;
We are no five-bob colonials – we are the 'ome-made supply,'

The wild young Australians introduced Beira to Australian culture. They had a game called 'knock off hats' where the object was to knock off the hat of a friend. There were no rules other than that any damage inflicted should not be permanent. When the local police saw Lieutenant Richard Dines Doyle and three of his friends engaged in this activity they attempted to restore peace. After the inevitable confrontation the police force was securely parked beneath upended sentry boxes. With their day's amusement completed, the Australians returned to camp, stopping to pass a few minutes with their colonel.

Naturally the Portuguese authorities complained to the military, but the story was much magnified in the telling, so the three Australians became scores and their display of high spirits was altered to a major riot that endangered all Beira. It was lucky that the Australian colonel related the truth of events. After an apology by Doyle and his two companions, the incident was closed.

Some time later word spread that the Australian camp was to be visited by The Governor of Mozambique and Sofala. Naturally this created consternation and most of the Australian companies did their best to spruce up their lines. All sorts of devices were used, from pot plants to bunting, but Doyle and B Company only watched, slightly amused. They created an artificial bank, covered it with smooth grass and used white stones to spell out the words:

"B Company. Useful – Not Ornamental."

Apparently that display impressed His Excellency more than the elaborate ornamentation used by their sister companies.

Initially the Imperial troops intended to march to the relief of Mafeking. They advanced across Rhodesia, slaughtering the game and nearly killing one hapless man who sheltered behind a Baobab tree that was used for target practice. The hollow trunk of this tree proved no protection against rifle bullets.

Many of the Australians were seconded to other units and at one point in 1900 Doyle was sent to a British column that was scouring the veldt, looking for a Boer Commando. Sandhurst training might have been admirable for conventional warfare, but not for bush conflict. When the British subaltern in command rode unheedingly past an obvious set of tracks, Doyle pointed the fact out.

'How do you know that?' The Sandhurst man asked.

'There are tracks for five wagons and about a hundred men back there.' Doyle said.

'Can you track?' The British officer was amazed.

Like most Australian Bushmen, Doyle could. If Sandhurst men were not adept at bush warfare, they did have the advantage of connections, and before long Doyle had his own command.

This was nothing grand, perhaps forty hand-picked men, who had the distinction of small brass shoulder badges that boasted 'd a s' - Doyle's Australian Scouts. They were gathered informally, people recommending those they thought would be suitable for such an irregular formation. Although most came from the $1^{st}/4^{th}$ Imperial Bushmen, some joined from other formations, occasionally non-Australian. This elite band were attached to the staff of General Walter Kitchener, brother of Herbert Kitchener of Khartoum and such was the skill of Doyle that only one of their number was killed during the war. At a time of unfailing orthodoxy, Doyle was unorthodox.

The British Army was extremely traditional, both in regimental function and name. The infantry was the backbone, the cavalry the elite, used for mass charges or for completing the rout of broken troops. As neither had been used for reconnoitring an enemy, other units had to be formed for this purpose. The various scouting components were used to ensure that the British columns did not march into an ambush. In the veldt, with its undulations interspersed by kopjes and river valleys, the British were vulnerable to the fast moving and bush wise Boers. A score of Boer riflemen occupying a kopje could hold up an entire column for hours, inflicting numerous casualties. When the relatively ponderous British opened their ranks and advanced, the Boers would mount their horses and gallop away, to occupy the next kopje. The Scouts' primary function was to prevent this happening.

Doyle's Scouts operated far in advance of the Column. To test a position for the enemy, they had to approach and draw the Boer fire. If they suspected that not all the enemy had revealed themselves, they made a mock attack, estimated the number of rifles firing at them then withdrew.

The Scouts were Mounted Infantry, split into sections. There were eight men in a section, four in a half section and number four was the horseholder. When the men had dismounted to skirmish forward, the number fours held the reins. In their first operation, one of the men forgot to hand his reins to the horseholder and instead threw them over a thorn bush. When the shooting started the horse panicked and bolted, leaving his rider stranded in front of the Boer rifles. Lieutenant Doyle was already fifty yards away when he recognised he was a man short. Swearing fluently, he returned to rescue the man, too angry to realise that they were under fire.

As the campaign progressed, Doyle picked up pieces of useful field lore. He learned never to ride a distinctive horse, as the Boers would think this a fine target. It was also inadvisable to flinch if a long-range shot passed close. The marksman would certainly be watching and if he saw no reaction, would hopefully assume that his shot was unnoticed and therefore inaccurate. He would then adjust his range and fire either short or over. It appears obvious that Lieutenant Doyle took his soldiering seriously, but he did not follow the conventions of the British military.

Most British field officers led from the front. They marched, or at least rode, alongside their men, ensured that the horses were cared for first, then the men and lastly themselves. They would never sleep if their men were awake. Doyle was different. When on patrol he positioned his men, checked them and then left the NCOs in charge. Doyle left standing orders to call him at first light and, presumably, if there was any contact with the enemy. Then he went to sleep. His theory was simple. He had the responsibility for the lives of all his men and it was his duty to be alert and efficient. A tired man was neither. Perhaps it was this attitude that kept his casualty list so low; it was certainly this attitude that created friction between Doyle and those with higher military rank. All the same, Doyle was promoted, to Captain, and he kept his command, augmented with more men.

Interestingly, Montgomery also insisted on a good night's sleep while at the front in the Second World War.

Most of Doyle's reminiscences were episodic and it is unfortunately impossible to give a time or date for them. On one occasion the Scouts led a column through an affluent farm with a selection of beehives at the end of an avenue of trees. These beehives were positioned on top of posts, and as the Scouts passed, the last man prodded the last hive with his Martini-Henry carbine. Naturally the bees took offence and it was unfortunate that the staff officers immediately behind included a general riding a nervous horse. It took two days to repair the damage done by hundreds of bee stings, to repair damaged wagons and to reform the column.

There were occasions when the Boer marksmanship could be astonishingly accurate. When Doyle was on an exposed ridge relaying a message by heliograph, he noticed a group of Boers rising from the crest of another ridge about a mile distant. When one of the Boers appeared to prepare to fire his rifle, the Australians ignored him. The range was well over a mile, an impossible distance for even a Boer marksman. Within minutes a bullet flicked above their heads. Still the Australians did nothing, for the shot was obviously a fluke. The second fluke kicked up the dirt between the tripod legs of the heliograph and after the third fluke the Australians made a rapid withdrawal.

A marksman like that had to be seen, so Doyle sent up flanking parties who rounded him up. Perhaps it was not surprising that he should be elderly, with a white beard that stretched down his chest. When Doyle examined his rifle, he found it was a single-shot 1877 vintage Steyr with a drop-block breech and a long barrel sighted up to 2500 yards. Checking the distance, Doyle found the marksman had fired from 2300 yards.

On another occasion Doyle had completed an inspection of a kopje near Swartruggens in the Western Transvaal. As no Boers were found, Doyle stood on the summit, examining the area through his field glasses when somebody fired at him from about thirty yards away. A gun-to-gun duel began, Doyle with his carbine and the Boer with a Mauser. Doyle shot the Boer through the shoulder and when his Scouts came up in support they flushed a dozen Boers from the kopje. The Mauser was retained as a trophy of war.

On another occasion Doyle was leading a small group of Scouts near the Vaal River when they met a commando of Boers. Neither party had known of the other until they met head on, so the resulting firefight was brief, brisk and erratic. One of Doyle's pistol shots hit the neck of a horse ridden by one Brand Nussey, and the Boers were members of Smuts' Commando that eventually raided deep into the Cape Colony. In around 1923 the then Major R.D. Doyle D.S.O., J.P. met Nussey and the two became friendly. During this friendship, Doyle handed Nussey a photograph that he had captured at Klerkensdorp; the picture showed General De Wet, with Nussey in the foreground.

Unlike the tenacious but unimaginative British infantry, the Australians gained some fame for their ability for accurate firing while galloping forward. Doyle once explained how this came about. Prior to charging a supposed Boer position, the Scouts sent their best shots to the flanks to keep the enemy occupied while the remainder galloped forward, firing splendidly and shouting dramatically. Unaware of the marksmen on the flanks the Boers would see the shooting, advancing men and be aware of the accurate fire on their position. Perhaps more of a conjuring trick than anything else, this skill seemed to convince the Boers that the Australians were superb marksmen.

Possibly because of such ingenuity, or merely from a commanding officer that cared for his men, Doyle's Australian Scouts hardly had a casualty during the entire campaign. When the Staff came to hear of this, they made enquiries, apparently wondering if the Scouts were pressing home their attacks properly. During a war where one in every fifteen of the participants became a casualty, Doyle's statistics looked suspiciously meagre.

To rectify this, the Staff decided to send the Scouts on a frontal attack across a thousand yards of bare veldt against a position held by a suspected three hundred Boer riflemen. Doyle surveyed the ground before the advance took place, and noticed a copse of trees about half way between the Boer position and the British, but off to the side. After consultation with the artillery, an accurate barrage thundered around the Boer position, then Doyle galloped forward, not directly toward the Boers but to the trees. They rested there for a few minutes, to let the horses recover their wind, then charged the final, dangerous five hundred yards.

Almost at once a Maxim-Nordenfeldt opened up and the shellfire burst around the galloping Scouts, but when it jammed the Scouts pushed forward. By the time they reached the Boer position the enemy had decamped and again Doyle's Scouts had achieved a success without losing a man.

Out on the veldt the Scouts often met the local wildlife. If the big game had long been hunted to extinction, there was plenty bird life, including the Korhaan which was 'royal game' and sacrosanct to any hunter. This bird was as hated by the Scouts as was the lapwing to the Scottish Covenanters, and for nearly the identical reason. The Korhaan can conceal itself in rich grass or bare rock and tends to be busy on moonlit nights as well as during the day. Frequently when the Scouts were approaching a Boer position, slithering across the ground from cover to cover, a Korhaan would burst out of hiding with its noisy 'Kraak-krak-krak-krak!' With this alarm, the Boers could either escape or fight it out. Because of his experiences during the Boer War, Doyle retained a dislike for these birds and despite their official protection, shot them on sight. Apparently they are tough to eat, unless they are boiled for hours.

Perhaps meeting such wildlife encouraged the British soldiers when they created their campaign songs. As usual, these were either obscene or humorous or both, and would sound defeatist to anybody that did not know the character of the singer. One of these, written

111

down by Mr Douglas Doyle, son of Captain, later Major Doyle, was sung to the tune of the Eton Boating Song:

'Lovely trekking weather
Plenty of fowl and duck
Bullocks by the thousand
Sheep and goats and buck
But we've all got Mauseritis
We're off to the Cape in a truck
We've all got Mauseritis
We're off to the Cape in a truck.'

With or without defeatist songs, the British had to continue fighting even after the main Boer armies were vanquished. Kruger withdrew his Commando to Machadodorp and then vanished in the vast spaces of the north. The British believed, possibly correctly, that Kruger's intention was to divide his commando into small parties while being chased, then reform later.

Promoted to captain, Richard Doyle led his Scouts northward to the Escarpment to winkle out the scattered Commando. This was not an easy task, for these were the bitter-enders, the most wily guerrilla fighters of them all. The Scouts would follow the trail of any Boers they came across, but found it frustrating when the Boers gradually melted away. A group of twenty would decrease to ten, and then five, and then the trail would completely vanish.

This Northeast Transvaal territory is bad country where the Drakensberg sheers down into thick bush. In the early 1900s this was still big game country, and the Scouts would hear the angry cough of a leopard or the terrifying roar of a lion. Fairly soon after the Scouts arrived, Captain Doyle sent half a dozen men up the side of a mountain while the remainder scoured the kloofs and corries for the enemy.

When one of the climbers upset a loose stone, he started an avalanche that thundered onto the Scouts below. The Scouts ran for the safety of the plain beneath, followed down by hundreds of boulders of various sizes and a few equally panicking Boers. After that incident the Scouts used this technique to pluck the Boers from their sanctuary, and if there were relatively few prisoners taken, the Scouts probably did better than other units that used more conventional methods.

Captain Doyle's Scouts became involved in at least one incident when the local African tribes decided to join in. This event occurred in the Western Transvaal and the tribesmen had raided the Boer farms. By this stage of the war many of the Boer men were either prisoners of war or casualties, so it is possible that only women and children occupied these farms. The tribesmen killed when they could, and apparently some of the women were raped and tortured first. Captain Doyle later commented that what he saw on the farms was worse than anything he had seen during the war. Doyle's Scouts herded the culprits into a valley and surrounded them. Once the warriors realised that they were outgunned and could not escape, they surrendered. Rather than shoot them, the Scouts took away their weapons and handed them to the appropriate authorities. The media did not report this incident, so either they did not learn of it, or the authorities silenced them.

Of all the South African tribes, the Zulus arguably have the most warlike reputation. In part this may be because of the two films about their exploits against the British, or because their early King Chaka created an Empire that lasted for three generations and incorporated dozens of smaller tribes.

When the Boers headed their wagons north and east to escape from British rule in Cape Colony, they made bitter contact with the Zulu impis. Right from the early days on 1838 when Piet Retief led the first of the Voortrekkers to meet Dingane at Mgungundlovu there was misunderstanding. Dingane, king of the Zulus, gave the identical parcel of land to both Boer and Briton, then massacred Retief and his party.

113

Two hundred and eighty one Boers were killed, together with about two hundred and fifty of their servants and around five hundred Zulus, but the Boers retaliated with a Commando. The Zulus repelled this near uThaleni, and followed this by defeating a British effort from Port Natal. It took another commando led by Andries Pretorius to avenge the Boers, and the ensuing battle of Blood River was a decisive Boer victory.

There were other battles, and if the Boers were not always victorious, they usually managed to give a good account of themselves. The Boers were farmers who demanded huge areas of land, and they believed that Africa was theirs by right. The Zulus, or any other native tribe, were not considered. So when the British-Boer War of 1899 started, it is not really surprising that the Zulus offered their assegais to help the British. The British rejected the offer politely, but the Zulus were a stubborn people and argued their case. They were persistent in their desire to help their British friends, but when it was explained to them that the British took prisoners in war and the Zulus did not, the warrior tribesmen departed.

It was a few months later that the British headquarters in Pietermaritzburg was surprised to find a small body of Zulus trotting through the town. In the midst of them was a Boer, wounded and exhausted. The impi of Dinizulu were well pleased with their success and boasted that they had indeed taken a prisoner: here was the proof. The British still turned down their offer of help.

Apparently a small unit detached from the impi had met half a dozen Boers who were riding from Northern Natal to join Louis Botha. In the ensuing sharp fight, all the Boers had been killed save a man named Engelbrecht, who was captured. After the war, Engelbrecht took over the farm of Maroelaskop, not far from Nylstrom on the Springbok Flats. His sons and grandsons became excellent shots, continuing the Boer tradition.

After the peace came the disbanding and Doyle's Scouts were relegated to less than a footnote of history. The Australians had done their bit, helped add another chunk to the Empire and their grateful King provided two ships to sail them home. They embarked at Durban, with the other ranks along the taffrail, cheerfully watching their ex-officers struggling to step into heaving small boats. Most fell during the attempt, to sprawl in an undignified and unsoldierly manner across the thwarts.

Doyle was also watching, and realised that a seaman with a megaphone was shouting 'Now!' to the officers, who chose to ignore his advice. Doyle did not. Even although the small boat was dozens of feet beneath him when the call came, he stepped faithfully forward, and the boat rose with the waves. Doyle was the first officer to enter the boat on two legs.

In 1904 he was back in South Africa, purchasing a farm in the Great Karoo, paying three shillings and sixpence (17.5 pence) an acre. He worked in the Waterberg District of the Transvaal, trying to re-establish farmers on farms that been systematically destroyed on the orders of Lord Kitchener. In 1906 he was awarded the DSO and celebrated with a wild party.

If Doyle's Australian Scouts only lasted for the duration of the war, another formation had a longer, and equally distinguished history. When Kitchener declared that he wanted fighting men who could ride, the Caledonian Society of Johannesburg offered to recruit from Scottish South Africans, with the unit being known as The Scottish Horse. This offer was accepted and command was given to Captain and Brevet Major the Marquis of Tullibardine, D.S.O. Possibly revealing his knowledge of Walter Scott, Kitchener ordered Tullibardine to 'send out the fiery cross', which was an old Highland method of gathering fighting men for a campaign.

By February 1901 the Scottish Horse numbered four fighting squadrons, with fifty African, primarily Zulu, scouts and fifty bicyclists. After training at Maritzburg, they worked with Kekewich's column in the Western Transvaal. They had a busy time, riding hard and fighting many skirmishes and three larger battles.

The first of these was at Moedwil on 30th September 1901 when the Scottish Horse helped repel a Boer attack on the column at the cost of 73 casualties. The second was the successful capture of Sarel Albert's commando at Gruisfontein and the third at Roodewal in April 1902 when Kemp attacked the column. This was perhaps the last open battle of the war as over one thousand Boers, led by Potgieter in a blue shirt, fired from the saddle as they charged knee to knee at Kekewich's column. It was a bright day, no rain, no wind and the British, aided by six field guns and two pom-poms, sent them staggering back. Potgieter was killed seventy yards from the Scottish Horse position.

By that time the Scottish Horse was perhaps more imperial than any other unit, yet still retained its Scottish character. Dressed in khaki, they wore a blackcock's tail in the broad brimmed hat they sported, and in March 250 Scots-Australians reinforced them. As may be imagined, these Australian Scots had an independent attitude that nearly amounted to bloody mindedness, and they merged easily with the 400 home born Scots recruits to form a second battalion. So independent was this regiment that it answered only to Tullibardine, not to the Yeomanry authorities.

While most of the columns were huge, ponderous affairs that rolled over the veldt, there were a few smaller, faster independent 'search and destroy' columns. Lieutenant Colonel George Elliot Benson of the Royal Artillery commanded the most successful of these. His intelligence officer, Aubrey Wools-Sampson, who already had an interesting history, aided Benson. Wools-Sampson had fought in the Zulu War, endured capture and torture by the Bapedi and had survived a Boer bullet in the First Boer War. Not content with retirement, he had ridden in the Jameson Raid and was wounded again at Elandslaagte. He made extensive use of native scouts, did not mix with the other officers and loathed the Boers.

Perhaps it was because of their fighting ability that the second battalion of Scottish Horse was sent to join Benson's column. In all there were four artillery pieces, two pom-poms and 1400 men, Scots,

English, South Africans and the inevitable Australians. In July, Lieutenant English won the Victoria Cross at Vlakfontein when 26 men of the Scottish Horse fought off 63 Boers.

So used to attacking the British, the Boers were frequently caught without sentries, and once the scouts located their laagers, Benson's men attacked at night or at dawn. The Boers learned not to remain in the same place on two consecutive nights and even de Wet said of this British innovation '...these night attacks were the most difficult of the enemy's tactics with which we had to deal.'

Louis Botha led the Boers in this sector of the central and eastern Transvaal and on the 7th September 1901 he led two thousand men in an invasion of Natal. Kitchener ordered four of his huge columns to crush Botha, but first contact was on September 17th when Lt-Colonel Gough led less than three hundred men in a disastrous cavalry charge against Botha's commando. Kitchener responded by sending more men.

Botha fell on two British positions, Fort Itala and Fort Prospect, which guarded the border between Transvaal and Zululand. He called on the garrisons to surrender and a Durham collier at Prospect gave a classic reply 'I'm a pitman at home and I've been in deeper holes than this before.' Both forts held out and Botha withdrew to the veldt. It was now that Commandant Grobler sent a message from Brakenlaagte that he was skirmishing with Benson's column and Botha rushed over with reinforcements.

On a wet 30th October 1901 Benson was returning to the railway for supplies. With Grobler's commando harassing him, Benson had difficulty fording a drift, particularly when his pom-pom jammed. However his rearguard seemed to be coping with the Boer attacks. Only when Botha appeared did Benson lead two squadrons of the Scottish Horse to reinforce the rearguard, and then Botha charged. As well as the two squadrons of the Scottish horse there were two guns of the 84th battery and men of the Yorkshire Light Infantry, the

King's Royal Rifle Corps, the East Kent Regiment and the North Lancashire Regiment. They were outnumbered 7 to 1 by the Boers.

Withdrawing to a low kopje, they fought on a through a misty day, sniping with the Boers until they ran out of ammunition, then snapping home the bayonet until the Boers should close. Quartermaster Sergeant Warnock of the Scottish Horse, a veteran of 21 years with the Kings Own Scottish Borderers brought ammunition to the riflemen and fought on until he was wounded three times.

'Surrender!' demanded Botha's men.

'We're Scots,' came the reply, together with a volley of Lee-Enfield bullets.

By now Benson was wounded three times. When the Boers charged the British met them with the bayonet, but they were too heavily outnumbered. When the Boers took the kopje, British artillery fired on the position, and the Boers withdrew. They returned at night and dragged away the captured guns.

At the beginning of the action there were 79 officers and men of the Scottish Horse, but by the time the fighting ended only six remained unwounded. Although the guns were captured and Benson killed, the rest of the column escaped, and after the war one of the gun carriages was handed to Tullibardine. It still stands outside Blair Castle in Perthshire.

By this stage of the war, the British and Colonials were as skilled as the Boers in veldt fighting. When the recruits joined the ranks of the veteran units they were given short advice to keep clear of officers and white rocks. The Boer marksmen always singled out the officers, and light coloured rocks were used as ranging marks.

When peace came, men of the Scottish Horse took part in the Coronation procession of the new King Edward. They were described as Tullibardine's Desperadoes, and they rode with the blackcock's feather as jaunty in the streets of London as it had ever been on the veldt.

Chapter 13 : A Gathering Of Generals

The Boer war was not characterised by brilliant generalship, although a number of generals, such as French, Macdonald and Haig, enhanced their reputations. Others, such as Lord Roberts and Kitchener, maintained their position in the public eye, while Redvers Buller suffered official reproach. In this chapter, the actions of some of the leading British officers will be outlined.

Of all the British general officers that fought in the Boer War, only Hector Macdonald had risen from the ranks. He was arguably the source of more stories, legends and anecdotes than any other British officer of the period. Born the son of a small farmer and stonemason near Dingwall in the Black Isle in 1853, his military career reads like a book on late Victorian Imperial expansion. After enlisting as a private soldier in the Gordon Highlanders in 1870, he rose to colour sergeant by 1879, at which date he took part in the Second Afghan War. The Afghans held a strong position at Hazar Darakht, but Macdonald led 63 men above them and attacked, throwing the Afghans back. According to folklore Lord Roberts offered Macdonald either a commission or a Victoria Cross. Macdonald took the field commission, stating that he would win the Victoria Cross later. It was a decision that saw him rise to fame, but also one that ultimately led to his death. From that date Macdonald was to be ever in the public eye as he fought his way through Africa.

In 1881 he displayed splendid bravery at the Battle of Majuba Hill during the First Boer War. The British had invaded Boer territory and on 26 February Major-General Sir George Colley led 650 men, including 180 of the Gordon Highlanders, up Majuba Hill. They arrived by dawn and, although Lieutenant Ian Hamilton and Colonel Macgregor believed that they should dig in, Colley stated that the hill was too formidable for the Boers to storm. However, the Boers attacked, keeping under cover of the various rocks that were strewn over the slopes, and firing constantly. With the Boers far better shots than the British, the defenders retreated in one of the most humiliating defeats suffered by Victorian Britain. Colley was quickly killed, but Second Lieutenant Macdonald refused to either retreat or surrender. Out of ammunition, he threw rocks at the Boers, and when they closed, fought with his fists. It took several Boers to overpower him, with one saying 'this man is too good to kill.' Held prisoner for a while, Macdonald was later returned to the British army.

In 1885 he was involved in the attempt to rescue the beleaguered General Gordon in Khartoum. Still in North Africa, he fought in the battle of Suakin in the Sudan in 1888 and was awarded the DSO the following year. After fighting at Tokar in the Sudan in 1891, he led the Second Infantry Brigade on the Dongala Expeditionary Force of 1896.

Two years later Kitchener invaded the Sudan with 25,000 troops, of whom over 8000 were British. His objective was the capture of Omdurman and Khartoum. While camped at Omdurman, the Dervish army attacked, to be sent back with some 2000 casualties. Kitchener then ordered an advance on Khartoum, leaving Macdonald with his 3000 Sudanese and Egyptians in reserve. However, an officer of the Camel Corps informed Macdonald that some 20,000 Dervishes were approaching the British army, then marching in vulnerable columns. Despite Kitchener's orders to join the march, Macdonald advanced to face the Dervish army. Eventually Kitchener realised that there was a real danger in his rear and returned to the fight. It was Macdonald, however, who saved the day and became the hero of Omdurman. When the battle was finally won, some of his men had only two bullets remaining. Later that year Macdonald became Aide de Camp to Queen Victoria.

After a spell as Brigadier–General in India, Macdonald returned to Africa in January 1900, when the Highland Brigade was licking its wounds after the mauling at Magersfontein. Macdonald took command at the Modder River Camp. He addressed the assembled men, and introduced them to his unique style of leadership by taking command of an individual company. He also spoke to each Scottish battalion, every officer and many of the non-commissioned officers and men. He told them that Lord Roberts was now in overall command and that things would improve. Macdonald showed concern for the food, recreation and equipment of the men, and ordered a series of parades to remind them that they were still expected to have a smart military appearance. He also visited the sergeant's mess and shook hands with the ordinary soldiers, raising the morale of the Highlanders.

After a successful skirmish at Koodosberg, Macdonald led his brigade to the battle of Paardeberg, where Kitchener had temporarily taken over command from Lord Roberts. The Boers under Cronje were strongly entrenched in a wagon laager, surrounded by the British army. Obeying Kitchener's orders to advance over open ground, the Highlanders were caught by Boer fire but retained their position. Macdonald was one of the wounded. When Roberts reassumed command, the Highlanders told him the position of the Boer riflemen, so the artillery could inflict major damage.

A misunderstood message led the British to believe that Cronje intended to surrender, but when the British marched forward to the laager, rifle fire decimated them. The artillery again opened up and on 27th February, the anniversary of Majuba, Cronje surrendered. It was the first major victory for the British in the war.

After Paardeberg, Roberts began his victorious march into the Boer Republics, with Macdonald at his side. Macdonald was ordered to clear an area of the Orange Free State of the Boers, which proved a daunting task for his infantry. Christian de Wet captured a convoy and 150 Black Watch in June 1900, and another hundred Highlanders at Honing Spruit in July, but the next month Macdonald was instrumental in the important action at Brandwater Basin, when over 4000 Boers were captured. There was a further victory at Brantford, north of Bloemfontein, but perhaps Macdonald's character was best revealed during the later, farm-burning phase of the campaign. While soldiers were destroying the property and stock of the de Kok family, the young son of the family appealed to him for help. At once he wrote a quick note 'Don't interfere with these cows – Hector Macdonald, General.' He spoke of his men as 'Poor fellows, the work is hard, hard indeed...but they are always cheery and never complain.' Macdonald seemed lacking in the attitudes that separated officers from men, even wearing uniform without insignia. On one occasion the Canadian Lt Morrison spent some time speaking with him on a railway platform before realising that the soldier was indeed General Macdonald.

In 1901, Macdonald was knighted and the following year was ordered to command the army in Ceylon. At this time the class system was in full control, particularly in such outposts of Empire, and the local civilian authorities resented this man of 'low breeding' gaining command. Governor Sir J. West Ridgeway seemed to be the leading voice among those who wished Macdonald removed, and it has been alleged that he encouraged the spate of newspaper letters that accused Macdonald of homosexual tendencies, at that time a crime. The letters stated that a man of Macdonald's age should have a wife and children, and alleged that he had no liking for ladies. Ridgeway asked Macdonald to either leave the island or face a court martial, but when Macdonald spoke to King Edward, he was promptly ordered back.

General Macdonald reached Paris, where he realised that the allegations had spread beyond Ceylon to the entire world. Riddled with dysentery, with his general health poor and suffering from depression, Macdonald committed suicide with his own pistol. What Afghans, Dervish and Boers could not do, the British class system and intense jealousy had performed, driving a brave man to his death. Ironically, it was Macdonald's wife who came to claim the body. He had been married to Christina MacLouchlan from Edinburgh since 1884, with their son, Hector Duncan Macdonald, born in 1887. Because Kitchener did not approve of his officers marrying, and with the Duncan family frowning on the match, the marriage had been kept a secret.

Interestingly, many in Scotland believed that Macdonald was not dead, but had secretly joined the German army, taking the identity of

August von Mackensen, a distinguished officer of similar age and appearance. During the First World War the Germans capitalised on this belief, dropping propaganda leaflets on the British lines boasting of the conversion of a Scot to the German cause. There appears no truth in the legend, but it does reveal the depth of feeling for a popular soldier.

There were different feelings for Horatio Herbert Kitchener, a man whose portrait, plastered on a poster, was to grace walls throughout Britain. Kitchener is probably best remembered for the poster of the First World War where he announces that 'Your Country Needs You', yet his military career was founded on his exploits in the Sudan during the previous century and he played an important part in the British-Boer War. In common with so many British soldiers, Kitchener was Irish, born in County Kerry in 1850. After an education at the Royal Military Academy at Woolwich and a spell in the French Army, he was commissioned into the Royal Engineers in 1871 but found garrison life boring so became a surveyor in Palestine, before serving in Cyprus. Attached to the Egyptian Army, Kitchener was involved in the abortive attempt to relieve Charles Gordon, who was under siege from the Mahdist armies in Khartoum. In 1886 Kitchener became Governor of Britain's Red Sea Territories and helped repel a Mahdist invasion of Egypt. By 1892 he was commander in chief of the Egyptian Army, which he reorganised and modernised, then built a railway along the Nile to prepare for the reconquest of the Sudan.

It was not until 1898 that Kitchener became a household name, when his armies conquered the Sudan from the Mahdi's Dervishes. After victory at the battle of Omdurman he became Lord Kitchener, although popularly known as Kitchener of Khartoum or K of K. That same year he blocked a French attempt to claim the territory in the celebrated Fashoda Incident, which had the potential to lead to war between Britain and France.

Arriving in South Africa as chief of staff to Lord Roberts, Kitchener failed in his frontal attack on Paardeberg. When Roberts returned to Britain, Kitchener was left with the difficult task of quelling the Boer commandoes in their effective guerrilla campaign. His strategy of farm burning, while moving the civilian population to internment camps, was perhaps the most controversial decision of the war. However, Kitchener's use of fortified blockhouses eventually helped defeat the mobile Boer commandoes. Kitchener was also a genuinely courageous man. After the first few weeks of the war, the British had learned that riding a horse of any distinctive colour invited a Boer bullet. However, Kitchener deliberately flouted the convention of appearing anonymous by riding a white horse, even when at the head of his army.

When the Treaty of Vereeningen ended the Boer war in 1902, Kitchener was appointed commander-in-chief in India, a position he held until 1909, and then returned to Egypt as military governor. In 1914, with the outbreak of the First World War, the Prime Minister, Herbert Asquith, appointed Kitchener, now an Earl as Secretary of War, with the immediate task of raising an army large enough for modern European War. Kitchener achieved this, recruiting 3,000,000 volunteers in two years with the help of an advertising campaign. Asquith said that he was not a great man, but 'a great poster.' Indeed, his greatest contribution to the First World War was his recruitment of millions by his reputation.

Although Kitchener's methods had been criticised in South Africa, he was correct in his prediction that the First World War would last for at least three years, with terrible casualties, and he believed that the main effort should be in France. However, he did bow to the First Lord of the Admiralty, when Winston Churchill persuaded him to send hundreds of thousands of men to Gallipoli in early 1915. The campaign turned into a bloodbath with a quarter of a million allied casualties and no reward.

With his reputation diminishing, Kitchener was also blamed for a lack of military supplies. Conan Doyle thought him arrogant and stupid, with no idea about munitions, no belief in tanks and a bias against Irish and Welsh divisions. Kitchener was also blamed for using Boer-war era shrapnel rather than high explosive, which could have blasted away the German trenches. His offer to resign was refused, presumably because the British public continued to hold him in high regard, but in the spring of 1916 Asquith sent him to Russia to raise the morale of that nation. On 5th June, his ship, HMS *Hampshire,* was mined off Orkney and Kitchener drowned.

A big man, monosyllabic, taciturn, he was never a team player, but his personality was vital in both the Boer and the First World War. He was a noted Freemason, holding high office in Britain, North Africa and India, a fact that may add credence to the legend of Boer farms that were adorned with Masonic symbols being left severely alone. However, there is a persistent legend in Orkney that when the *Hampshire* went down, local boatmen were prevented from going to his rescue. Perhaps the powers that be believed that Kitchener had achieved all that he could, and that he was becoming a liability. Certainly he was an unusual popular hero, being ruthless, arrogant, energetic and a known looter with no regard for women.

In total contrast to Kitchener, Field Marshall Lord Roberts of Kandahar was one of the most successful and popular British soldiers of the period. 'Bobs' Roberts made his reputation in Afghanistan and confirmed it in South Africa two decades later. Born in Cawnpore, India, he was educated at Eton, Sandhurst and Addiscombe before entering the Bengal Artillery in 1851. He saw much action during the Indian Mutiny, taking part in the siege of Delhi, the relief of Lucknow and winning the Victoria Cross at Khudagani in 1858.

Roberts was present during the 1863 Umbeyla campaign, became assistant quartermaster general during the highly successful Abyssinian campaign of 1868, took part in the Lushai expedition of 1871-72 and was a major-general by 1878 when the Second Afghan War erupted. Roberts' Afghan service was one of constant victory. After defeating the Afghans at Peiwar Kotal and Charasia, he occupied Kabul and governed the country. However, it was not until August 1880 that he performed the astounding Kabul to Kandahar march with 10,000 men that ensured his reputation, following up the march with a splendid victory over Ayub Khan.

In 1881 Roberts became commander-in-chief of the Madras Army, then was promoted to command the army in India from 1885 to 1892. With the British Army split by rivalry between the 'African' branch, personified by Garnet Wolseley, and the 'Indian' branch, Roberts still rose to the top. Further promotion followed, and after a spell as commander in chief in Ireland, in 1899 he was sent to South Africa, where the Boer War was going horribly wrong. By this time Roberts was known as 'Bobs' or 'Kipling's General' and was known for his care for his men as much as his shrewd tactics.

Lord Roberts had a personal interest in the war, for his son Frederick had been killed at the battle of Colenso performing an act for which he was posthumously awarded the Victoria Cross, but, with Bobs in charge, the British soldier knew there would be no more disasters. Lord Roberts was not one to launch suicidal frontal attacks against massed riflemen. He arrived at Cape Town on the 10th January 1900, reorganised the army and was in overall command when the sieges of Ladysmith and Kimberley were raised, but was sick during the first part of the battle of Paardeberg, when Kitchener reverted to the frontal attack.

Finally victorious at Paardeberg, Roberts captured Bloemfontein, Johannesburg and Pretoria, sweeping aside all Boer opposition with a serious of flanking movements. When Mafeking was relieved, Britain exploded into paroxysms of glee while the defender, Baden-Powell was raised into something of a cult figure. This phase of the war is remembered not for military victories, but for tactical skill as Roberts organised and led a large army on marches through unorganised and enemy-occupied territory, in African heat and with disease in the ranks. When the last organised Boer army was smashed at Bergendal in August 27th, and the country occupied, Roberts annexed the Boer territories to the Empire. In November he handed control over to Kitchener and became an earl and Commander in Chief of the Army. He retired in 1904, but made a trip to the trenches in France in 1914, where he died while visiting the troops.

Roberts was known for his self-aggrandisement and, aware that Europe would soon be at war, advocated conscription. His men, for whom he showed affection and genuine concern, also universally loved him. Perhaps L.S. Amery, the editor of the *Times History of the War in South Africa,* was correct to term him 'the greatest British soldier of the century between Waterloo and the world wars.'

One of the commanders whose star rose during the Boer War was Sir John Pinkston French. Born in Ripple, Kent, in 1852, French gained fame as the dashing cavalry commander during the Boer War, but threw away his reputation in Flanders in 1914. At the age of 14 he had joined the Royal Navy, but transferred to the army eight years later. As an officer of the 19th Hussars, he fought through the Sudan Campaign of 1884 and 1885, and was a cavalry commander when the Boer War started.

French won a fine victory at Elandslaagte, where the Gordon Highlanders charged to the slogan 'Majuba!' and the lancers slaughtered the fleeing foe, but could not prevent the Boers besieging Ladysmith. He was made famous by the Great Flank March that finally relieved Kimberley, but at the expense of much of the horseflesh of the British Army. He shone in the manoeuvres to trap Cronje at Paardeberg and led his cavalry across the Vaal to invade the Transvaal. The British infantrymen knew him as 'the safety valve' and thought of him 'the terror of the Boers.' Others, less inclined to hero worship, knew him as a moody, erratic commander, but French's cavalry was seen as victorious, in contrast with the plodding, suffering infantry.

After the Boer War, French was promoted to Chief of the General Staff and then Field Marshall in 1913. He was in command of the British Expeditionary Force to France in 1914 and defended Ypres heroically but failed to create a good working relationship with his French allies. With no scope for his cavalry in the stalemate of trench warfare, French complained about the lack of shells and performed dismally at the Battle of Loos in 1915. He was replaced and sent to Ireland, where he managed the response to the Easter Rising. General French died in 1925, with his reputation battered by failure in the First World War, but nothing can diminish the memory of his defence of Ypres in 1914 or his frantic cavalry charges in South Africa.

As a contrast to General French, Sir Redvers Buller, was already a hero in 1899. Born in Crediton, Devon, Buller saw his reputation peak during the Zulu Wars, but fell from grace, perhaps unfairly, during the difficult operations in Natal during the Boer War. After an education at Eton, he bought a commission in the crack 60th Rifles in 1858, and fought in the China War of 1860 and the Red River Campaign in Canada in 1870. A member of the Wolseley Ring, he was in West Africa for the Ashanti War of 1874 and South Africa for the 1878 Kaffir War.

During the Zulu War of 1879 Buller gained the Victoria Cross for his bravery in rescuing two officers and a trooper during the action at Inhlobane. He remained in South Africa as chief of staff during the unsuccessful First Boer War of 1881, and fought in both Egypt and the Sudan in the 1880s, where he was promoted to major general.

By this time Buller was one of the military heroes of the late Victorian age. He was Commander in Chief of the forces in South Africa during the second Boer War, with 70,000 men, the largest army Britain had yet sent overseas. His first attempt at relieving Ladysmith ended in the disaster at Colenso, and his alleged suggestion that Sir George White, garrison commander, should surrender, seriously damaged Buller's reputation. 'The enemy is too strong for my force...I cannot break in' he said, and thought it best that White should fire away as much ammunition as possible and seek the best terms possible for surrender. That suggestion would never be forgotten.

Another attempt at relief ended in the battle of Spion Kop, where the British were again defeated, and again Buller had to shoulder some of the blame. A third attempt at relief was also unsuccessful, but Buller was known for his dogged determination. His army finally broke through the Boer lines, winning the nearly forgotten battle of Pieters Hill to relieve Ladysmith on 27th February 1900.

After criticism of Buller's methods, Roberts replaced him in overall command, although Buller remained in charge of the Natal Army. He persisted in driving the Boers from the rough country of the Biggarsberg, drove a passage through Lang's Nek and captured Lydenburg. These successes did something to restore his good name, but higher command had lost confidence in him. Buller returned to Britain and assumed responsibility for army training. There is no doubt that he was indecisive, and his tactical errors cost many lives. However, there is reason to believe that Buller had a raw deal, for his relief of Ladysmith encountered some of the toughest terrain of the war, and he has been credited with inventing the rolling barrage and short-rush tactics that eventually neutralised the sharp shooting of the Boers. Never disliked by his troops, crowds greeted Buller on his return to Aldershot in January 1901. He retired in October 1901 and died in 1908, remembered as the 'father' of the Army Service Corps.

The slaughter of the First World War ruined the reputation of Sir Douglas Haig, although at the time he was regarded as a hero who won the war. Born in Edinburgh in 1861, he was educated at Clifton and Oxford, entering Sandhurst in 1884. He shone at his military studies and was commissioned into the 7th Hussars, where he served nine years, mostly in India. After a brief spell as a staff officer to Colonel John French, and time spent in Staff College, he accompanied Kitchener to the Sudan in 1898. Haig fought at the Atbara and Omdurman, before being appointed a lieutenant-colonel on the staff of General French in South Africa.

Haig's bravery was never in doubt as he was mentioned in despatches four times during the Boer War, where he also commanded the 17th Lancers. Returning to Britain in 1902, he became a brevet colonel and was awarded the CB. After holding various prestigious staff appointments, in 1914 he commanded 1 Corps, half the original British Expeditionary Force. He gained command of the First Army on Christmas 1914, and led it through the climatic battles of Loos and Neuve Chapelle in 1915. In December of that year Haig took overall command of the British Army in France, a post he held until the Armistice of 1918. Despite political difficulties with Lloyd George which saw him working with fewer men than he would like, and a government strategy that saw the British Army sending men to pointless eastern theatres of war, Haig continued with the thankless and almost impossible task of battering at the German defences.

He led the army to the battles of the Somme, Arras and Passchendale, where he had to continue a slaughterhouse to conceal the fact that the French Army had mutinied. Haig had to accept an addition to the British defence lines that led to the front being under strength, but showed at his best during the German March attack of 1918. His 'backs to the wall' speech has something Churchillian in its determination not to accept defeat. It was Haig who suggested a single commander for the allies in France, and Haig who led the British Army to ultimate victory in 1918.

Created an Earl, Haig has since become a controversial figure. While some think him a blunderer who wasted hundreds of thousands of lives, others point out that he was using the best military strategy then known, and his war of attrition did defeat the German Army. However, he was a believer in the horse soldiering that had won the Boer War and liked neither the machine gun nor the tank. After the war he helped establish the Royal British Legion to care for the troops that he had commanded.

One of the least remembered of the Boer War generals, Ian Hamilton was born in Corfu in 1853. After his education, in 1870 he became one of the first officers to obtain a commission by examination, rather than by purchase. He spent a year in Germany, learning at first hand how militaristic that new nation was becoming, and then joined the Suffolk Regiment in Ireland before transferring to the Gordon Highlanders in India.

Hamilton fought in the Second Afghan War, then in the First Boer War, where he was wounded at Majuba Hill, and was declined the Victoria Cross on the grounds that he was too young. In February 1882 he became aide-de-camp to Sir Frederick Roberts in Madras, where he trained his troops in musketry and wrote *The Fighting of the Future*. Action with the Gordon Highlanders in the Sudan followed, then another spell of training troops in musketry in India. In 1895 Hamilton commanded a brigade in the Kohat Expedition, and in 1898 again fought on the North West Frontier. The following year saw him in South Africa, leading the 7th Brigade as a major general. He took part in the victory at Elandslaagte, where he again was refused a Victoria Cross, and fought at Wagon Hill during the siege of Ladysmith. Sent home with Roberts, Hamilton returned to Africa to act as Kitchener's chief of staff, with orders to privately report on the commander in chief's health.

After the Boer War, Hamilton was GOC of Southern Command in Britain in 1905, and Commander in Chief of Home Forces when the First World War broke out. His duties included raising reinforcements and home defence at a time when German invasion seemed a genuine possibility. Sent to command the landings at Gallipoli, Hamilton was under-resourced for a near-impossible task. His reputation suffered, although it is difficult to see what else he could have done. Relieved of command, he became Lieutenant of the Tower of London and died in 1948.

Taken together, the British generals of the Boer War were an undistinguished collection, who struggled to defeat a much smaller enemy. However, they had to use the resources and skills that they had, and fought a twentieth century guerrilla war with essentially nineteenth century weapons. If they failed, the fault was not their own, but the system that had created them.

Chapter 14 : A Brace Of Burghers

Despite all the strength of the British Empire that was pitted against them, despite the Highlanders and Yeomanry, the Imperial Bushmen and Strathcona's Horse, despite the skill of the New Zealanders and determinations of Rimmington's Tigers, the Boers fought on long after hope had died. With the majority of the burghers either in prison camps, dead or despondent, those that remained were the best, the hardest of hard liners. They called themselves the 'bitter enders.'

Of all the commandos that caused the British so many problems in the later stages of the war, that commanded by de Wet was probably the most effective. De Wet epitomised the skill and determination of the burghers; if the Boer republics were to be personalised into a single man, that man would be de Wet.

Born in October 1854 at Leeukop in the Smithfield district of the Orange Free State, Christiaan de Wet was the sixth of fourteen children. In common with many farm bred Boers, he received little schooling and was involved in running the family farm before his fourteenth birthday. When he was nineteen he married Cornelia Kruger, and worked as a transport rider in Griqua West. Settling on a Transvaal farm, he became a professional hunter and took an active part in the First Boer War – although he would have termed it the First War of Independence – in 1881. Acting as commandant of Heidelberg, he directed the Boer victory of Laings Nek, and fought at Ingogo and Majuba.

Seemingly unable to settle, de Wet moved from farm to farm, from Heidelberg to Lydenburg. He dabbled with politics, being elected to the Transvaal Volksraad in 1885, but soon returned to the Orange Free State, where he bought his father's old farm of Nieuwejaarsfontein. Within a few years he was on the move again, this time to the Heilbron district, and from 1889 he represented the Upper Modder River in the Free State parliament.

133

In October 1899, de Wet rode to war with three of his sons, Kotie, Christiaan and Isak. He left another thirteen children on the farm. Taking command of the Heilbron commando he won his first victory at Ladysmith, sometimes known as Nicholson's Nek, when with between 200 and 300 burghers he captured around 800 British soldiers. The defeat was more due to bad British officers than poor soldiering, for the Irish Fusiliers had hardly fired a shot and could not believe that they were ordered to surrender. Other soldiers, who had dared to fire at the enemy, had been ordered to 'cease fire!' British officers did not trust other ranks to fire except in volleys, and only then only after a direct order.

By December 1899 de Wet was a field-general, operating under Cronje. Always restless, he argued for an invasion of Cape Colony to disrupt the British railways and raise the Cape Burghers in revolt. If de Wet's invasion had been attempted at that stage of the war, when the British were reeling after a sequence of defeats, the Cape Burghers may well have risen, with unknown but possibly far-reaching consequences. Instead Roberts took command of the British army and trapped Cronje, with his 4000 men, at Paardeberg.

De Wet, however, was not Cronje. As French moved to relieve Kimberley, de Wet pounced on his supply wagons at Waterval on the Riet River. After capturing half the invaluable oxen, 170 wagons full of rations and cattle as food on the hoof and even rum, de Wet wasted precious time in looting the supplies rather than harassing the British. 'Our booty was enormous' he gloated, with reason. Attempting to relieve the situation at Paardeberg, he enabled some of the trapped Boers to escape by capturing Kitchener's Kopje, but a British counter attack forced him to make one of the miraculous escapes that were to make him famous.

With Cronje captured and the Boer armies much depleted and even more demoralised, President Steyn ordered de Wet to take command on all the Free State commandos. No longer able to contemplate a victorious invasion of the Cape, de Wet now faced a resurgent British Army, led by a vastly experienced general who had the full confidence of his men. De Wet, with his commandos crumbling under him, tried his best. Fortifying the kopjes at Poplar Grove, he waited for the attack. Roberts duly obliged, and if French had not paused to water his horses, he would have been perfectly placed to trap the fleeing Boers.

Despite some hard fighting to dislodge de la Rey at Driefontein, Roberts continued his march to Blomfontein, after which de Wet allowed his burghers a break. When General Piet Joubert complained, de Wet explained that Roberts would rest and recuperate at Bloemfontein, which is exactly what happened. Refreshed, de Wet's men regathered at the Sand River, and readied themselves to renew the war. De Wet took control, ordering the burghers to dump their wagons and introducing a harsh regime. De Wet had no time for the weak; he enforced his authority with the sjambok, kept his own council and trusted nobody save his own sons. Unpopular in his person, his men trusted his skill in strategy and battle.

Now, with the British in seeming total command of both republics, de Wet began the campaigns that were to make him a household name throughout the world. What Garibaldi was to Italy or Wallace to Scotland, de Wet became to the fighting free burghers of the veldt. Rather than sending his men on suicide missions against defended British bases, he chose the typical guerrilla tactic of hitting soft targets, but still inflicted defeats on British forces larger than his own.

Brigadier-General Broadwood was his first victim. De Wet took 1600 men, with artillery and a maxim machine-gun to capture the waterworks on the Modder River. The target may seem mundane, but it kept Bloemfontein supplied with water and was guarded by a mere two companies of British troops. However, just before de Wet arrived, General Broadwood had dropped in with about 1800 mounted infantry and cavalry. A master of the daring attack, de Wet promptly decided to capture the lot.

The battle of Sanna's Post, named after a tiny rail-side settlement, began when the Boer artillery outranged the British 12-pounders, then, despite much genuine bravery from the British, de Wet killed or wounded 159 soldiers and captured another 400 together with artillery and 83 supply wagons. De Wet also occupied the waterworks and followed up his success by snapping up another 470 British soldiers at Moster's Hoek. He was less successful at Wepener, where South Africans of the Cape Mounted Rifles and Brabant's Horse saw him off after a seventeen-day siege.

With de Wet fast becoming a folk legend to his own people and a bogeyman to every khaki-clad soldier in South Africa, he seemed only to increase his reputation. After he led 80 men in an attack on the 150 strong garrison of Roodewal and captured massive amounts of British supplies, the burghers again lost discipline in unrestrained looting. Many British objected when de Wet's men read and destroyed bags of mail, with Winston Churchill terming it 'a poor and spiteful thing.'

Kitchener retaliated by burning Boer farms close to the railway. De Wet's home was amongst the first to be destroyed. Kitchener also contemplated putting Boer hostages on British trains, but when the British public objected to the practice he rescinded the order. Agile as ever, de Wet escaped from General Archibald Hunter's net that captured Prinsloo and over 4000 men at the Brandwater Basin.

The unity of the burghers was crumbling, with 'handsuppers' who surrendered to the British now outnumbering those who continued the fight. Even de Wet's brother, General Piet de Wet became a scout for the British. De Wet, however, fought on. By now he was the main target of the British Army, and Roberts launched two columns in what was known as the First de Wet Hunt. Drawing British attention to himself so that Presidents Steyn and Kruger could escape, de Wet twisted free of his pursuers at Vredfort on the Vaal, split his men and thundered back toward the Free State until, forty miles west of Pretoria the British trapped him against the precipitous Magaliesberg range. When he was told that only baboons could cross it, de Wet stated 'where a baboon can cross, we can cross,' and clambered to safety.

As Roberts advanced to Komatipoort and dispersed the last of the Boer armies, de Wet helped restructure the Boers into smaller, hard riding commandos. To do so he called many of the erstwhile handsuppers back into action, disregarding their recent oath of neutrality to Britain. To the British this move was a blatant breach of the rules of war and, together with the Boer penchant for wearing captured British uniforms, encouraged their later programme of farm burning and concentration camps.

For a while de Wet's war slumped into a series of setbacks. His siege of Major-General Barton at Frederickstad in October failed, while Lieutenant-Colonel le Gallais nearly captured him in November at Doornkraal. Still undaunted, de Wet refused to listen to any talk of surrender and continued the war.

Invading the Cape Colony, de Wet captured a British garrison at Dewetsdorp. De Wet, however, again failed to bring about a rebellion of the Cape Dutch. When heavy rains impeded his horsemen and the British threw columns against him in the Second de Wet Hunt, he slipped through their fingers at Sprinkaansnek and returned north. He was back in the Colony for a third time in late January 1901, but again there was no rebellion by the Cape Dutch, who could work out which side was winning.

Now as the war entered its most desperate phase, Kitchener threw up lines of blockhouses, connected by wire. The blockhouses defended the railway and strategic river crossings, they thumped across the countryside, each one a minor strongpoint to delay and frustrate the Boer commandos. Then Kitchener organised a series of drives across the veldt, with British columns, each guided by units of irregular horse, pushing the commandos against the blockhouse lines. Each week the British totalled the number of Boers that they had 'bagged' in this grim facsimile of a pheasant shoot. However many Boers Kitchener captured, with Colonial and now better trained British horsemen tracking them across the brown grass and launching dawn strikes on unwary laagers, de Wet still remained loose.

Twisting and turning, de Wet slipped through gaps in the British line or inflicted losses in savage fights such as the skirmish at Groenkop near Harrismith. He remained free throughout 1901, but by March 1902 he knew that the end was near. Although he may have been able to avoid the British for years, the Afrikaner people were suffering. British military success, coupled with the farm burning and concentration camp system were ebbing their will to resist. Deputising as President of the Orange Free State de Wet signed the treaty of peace on the 31 May 1902.

Even after the war, de Wet continued to fight for his people. Only two months after the peace he was in Europe, campaigning for cash to help Boer widows and children, before he returned to politics. Only when the Union of South Africa united the two Boer republics with the English-speaking colonies did de Wet retire to his farm. In 1914, with South Africa supporting Britain in the First World War, de Wet protested against the invasion of German South West Africa. He joined the Afrikaner rebellion but was captured and sentenced to six years in jail and a hefty fine.

Reprieved after six months in prison, de Wet was never the same man. Retiring from public life, he spent the remainder of his life as a farmer until his death in 1923, but his memory has never died. His fame spread far from the Orange Free State, so that even King Edward mentioned him in casual conversation. When a desperate society woman was persistently seeking a match for her daughters, the King said 'they ought to set her to catch de Wet.' As one of the world's great patriots and guerrilla leaders, de Wet's name deserves to be remembered.

De Wet, however, was only one of a galaxy of burghers who battled against the British. De la Rey was another, Kruger yet one more, yet perhaps it is Daniel Theron who should be better remembered for symbolising the Boer people.

Theron's best-remembered exploit occurred during the siege of the laager at Paardeberg. Ranked as a captain, Theron volunteered to cross the British lines to enter the laager, and co-ordinate a Boer break out with General Cronje. Although the Boer War is better remembered for its use of horses, railways and balloons, Theron used a bicycle to approach the lines, but abandoned that to crawl through British troops near the Modder River. At one point a guard hailed him, and Theron engaged in conversation before continuing with his mission.

After meeting Cronje, Theron recrossed the British lines to inform De Wet that the general refused to countenance a break out. Even before the war, Theron was a firm believer in the use of bicycles, suggesting that he raise a cycling corps for the Transvaal, with horses reserved for fighting. The bicycle had certain advantages, Theron said, as it did not need sleep or fodder, while a piece of untanned leather inserted between tyre and tube would alleviate the problem of punctures. Granted permission, Theron established a bicycle corps manned by educated middle class Afrikaners. Armed with a revolver or carbine, the cyclists were used to carry messages, as Theron did in Natal when the heliograph between General Meyer and Erasmus was ineffective. Both sides also mounted bicycle patrols.

Theron's bicycle at Paardeberg was less easy for the British to see than a horse would have been, but despite this, Cronje still surrendered at Paardeberg. De Wet, however, recognised the bravery of Theron, saying 'he had performed an exploit unequalled in the war.' He also recognised inherent talent and allowed Theron to form the Theron Scouting Corps (*Theron se Verkenningskorps*). This formation was usually known as the TVK, but rather than bicycles, Theron reverted to the more traditional horse.

Theron's TVK became a legend among the Boers, as it targeted railway bridges and succeeded in capturing a number of British officers. According to the press, Lord Roberts termed Theron 'the chief thorn in the side of the British' and offered £1000 for his capture or death. In July 1900 General Broadwood led a force that attacked Theron, but the Boer escaped in a running skirmish that cost him eight dead and the British five.

Theron continued to harass the British, dynamiting the railway track, capturing trains and even freeing Boer prisoners from a British prison. At the beginning of September, Commandant Theron was near Fochville in the Gatsrand, contemplating an attack on a British column, when he encountered a patrol of Marshall's Horse. There was a skirmish, which brought more of the column's horse toward Theron. Trapped by horse and guns, Theron took refuge on a kopje, but British artillery killed him.

De Wet seemed genuinely moved by the loss of the scout. 'Where shall I find a man who combined so many virtues and good qualities in one person...Daniel Theron answered the highest demands that could be made on a warrior.' The Republic of South Africa later named a regiment and their School of Military Intelligence in his honour.

Chapter 15 : The Black Peoples

For a war supposedly between white men, there were many black people involved. At the beginning of the war Commandant Klaas Prinsloo commanded a sizeable force in the eastern Transvaal to overawe the Pedi while around 900 burghers guarded the Transvaal-Swaziland frontier. A similar number of men stood guard between the Orange Free State and Basutoland.

There were instances of combat between black Africans and the Boers. In November 1899 the Kgatla people attacked a Boer camp in the western Transvaal. A British supporting force quickly decamped, but this and similar incidents led to the Boers abandoning the area. In 1900 the Pedi mounted a guerrilla campaign against the Boers and regained their lands around Schoonoord and Ohrigstad. The Pedi horsemen of the eastern Transvaal, under their redoubtable chief Sekhukhune II frequently skirmished with the Boers. In autumn 1901 the Kgatla chief Lentshwe threw back a sizeable Boer commando from the Crocodile River. It has been estimated that the British employed and armed some 15,000 black Africans, who fought with the columns, while others manned the blockhouses or worked on the railways.

Of the two opponents, it was the British who mostly employed Africans as fighting men. Kgama, chief of the Ngwato mobilised around 1000 men to defend his sector of Bechuanaland, while Mfengu and Thembu tribesmen were used to defend the Transkei. Baden-Powell used black Africans in the defence of Mafeking, indeed when the Boers attacked on the 12th May 1900, it was the Baralong who did most of the fighting. The town of Herschel also had some 200 black Africans working as armed special constables. Swaziland, Bechuanaland, Basutoland and Zululand all had armed black men helping to defend the areas against Boer penetration. Others helped man the blockhouses.

However, the best-known example of black on Boer violence came from the Zulus. The Qulusi Zulu formed an impi that attacked the

Vryheid commando at Holkrans and killed 56 burghers. The veldt cornet, J. Potgeiter, was said to have received 45 assegai wounds. Those Zulus who were in the Natal and Zululand police force worked diligently throughout the war and Sergeant Gumbi of the Zululand Mounted Police was mentioned in despatches for his gallantry in leading a patrol through the Boer lines to assist in the defence of Fort Prospect in September 1901.

It is possible that the British did not utilise the full potential of the black military force because they believed it negligible. 'I need hardly say, there is no resemblance or analogy between the native tribes of South Africa and the native princes of India and their troops,' said A.J. Balfour to the House of Commons. There is also a strong possibility that the British, like the Boers, were afraid that arming large number of native Africans would lead to much future trouble. After all, it was just twenty years since a Zulu impi, armed with assegais, had soundly defeated a British army at Isandlwana. What would such warriors do when armed with more modern weapons?

However, both sides used native Africans.

The British transport riders were nearly exclusively native Africans. Many thousands of Africans worked as dispatch riders and message carriers, including through the Boer lines, and labourers. They worked as horse tenders and as general labourers. Many native Africans helped the British war effort, and often the British soldier thought more of them than he did of the white settler. Private Brown of the Argylls mentioned their friendliness and hospitality.

On commando, the Boers took native African servants. These people looked after the livestock, dug trenches, drove the carts and prepared food. Cronje used Tswanas to besiege the British in Mafeking, while armed Africans manned Boer outposts outside Ladysmith.

Blacks also suffered as non-combatants. During the siege of Mafeking, where the white defenders ensured that they themselves received the lion's share of the rations, several hundred black women attempted to escape to the nearby village of Kanya. The Boer intercepted them and, according to contemporary reports, stripped, and then whipped them before sending them back. Commandant Snyman of the Boer besiegers complained that Baden Powell was using 'the barbarians' to 'plunder, rob and murder.' Baden Powell replied that 'there are a number of natives about the country in a destitute condition owing to their homes having been burned and their cattle stolen by your burghers.'

Lady Sarah Wilson, who wrote for the *Daily Mail* during the siege of Mafeking, also mentioned the black population. In April 1900 she reported that a plague of locusts descended on the town and 'the natives gathered sacks full, and feed on them till their stomachs project in prominence of plentitude.'

Although there was no large scale black African invasion Africans did in many cases take advantage of the war. Some land was re-occupied, blacks frequently refused to labour for the whites and there was much cattle raiding, particularly when the white men were away to the war.

Most of the black people who took part in the war will remain forever anonymous, but the name of James Molife deserves to be better remembered. While Danie Theron is a Boer hero because of his exploit in crossing the British lines at Paardeberg, James Molife crossed the Boer lines at Ladysmith on no less than three occasions. A native runner, he carried important documents to and from the besieged, in the certain knowledge that if caught, he would probably be shot. Theron had no such worries.

Black Africans, however also suffered due to the British scorched earth policy. When the Boer women and children were transported to concentration camps, the black servants and workers were also taken away. Records show concentration camps for blacks in the former free republics and in Natal. Between 11500 and 14000 black Africans were held at these camps at any one time, with an estimated 14154 deaths, mainly of children. Black people caught up in the Boer siege of Kimberley suffered through scurvy when vegetables ran short.

The memorial to the Scottish Horse in Dunkeld Cathedral includes the names of the Zulu guides that died in action. They were an important and integral part of that formation. As the Boers tended to shoot Africans suspected of working for the British, it became normal for the scouts who were attached to the British formations in the latter, guerrilla, stage of the war, to carry rifles.

Many of the educated black peoples had hoped that a British victory over the Boer would lead to better conditions and possibly even enfranchisement. This was not to be. The British did nothing to alleviate the conditions of the black people in the former Boer republics, and this lack of action created bitterness. It seemed that the efforts of thousands of black people had been wasted.

Chapter 16 : Results Of The War

The war cost Britain over £200 million, a colossal amount in the early 20th century. More importantly over 400,000 horses, donkeys and mules died and out of the 365,693 British and Imperial and 82,742 colonial soldiers, over 100,000 became casualties. Of the nearly 22,000 who died, 5,774 were killed by enemy action and 16168 died of wounds or disease. Out of 87,365 Boers and mercenaries 7,000 died. An estimated 26,370 Boers died in the concentration camps. There were at least 7,000 Africans dead and perhaps as many as 12,000.

In 1906 the Transvaal became a self-governing colony, followed in 1907 by the Orange Free State. Only three years later both joined with Cape Colony and Natal to become the Union of South Africa. A new nation had been born from the bloodshed. In Britain, the government was alarmed at the effort it had taken to subdue a few thousand armed horsemen, particularly with Europe coalescing into armed camps. A re-organisation of the army took place, with much emphasis on musketry and marksmanship.

The standard of fitness and physique of many of the new recruits had been appallingly low so the government took dramatic action, including the provision of free school milk to build up the poorer children. In Manchester, three fifths of all volunteers had been unfit, even by the low standards of the army. In that racist era, people began to question if the British race was deteriorating due to industrialisation and urban life. It was a Quaker pacifist, Seebohm Rowntree, who suggested a connection between poverty and physical weakness. Eventually the debate would lead to better school meals for the worst off. The war also encouraged a new movement in outdoor recreation, with Baden-Powell's scouts at the forefront of a new idea of youthful activity, becoming a world-wide movement.

The Boer War advanced the development of military technology. The railway was important to both Boer and Briton – indeed the first blockhouses were built to protect the rail network. Steam traction engines were used to pull wagons, telegraphy became vital and many blockhouses were equipped with telephones. Searchlights were used, together with electric lighting, and the use of barbed wire and trenches became commonplace. By the end of the war British infantry at last altered its practice of advancing shoulder to shoulder, and British cavalry largely abandoned the use of the lance.

Possibly the most important lesson of the war was that modern smokeless magazine rifles combined with barbed wire and trenches meant that defence was easier than attack. Many theorists, however, saw in the mobility of the Boers the opposite lesson. Future wars, they believed, would be fast, with defensive earthworks avoided.

Many young officers who fought the Boers were high ranking Generals in the Great War, but, as so often, they had to re-learn the lessons, Names such as French, Haig, Kitchener and Hamilton were heard in the dark days of 1914 to 1918, and the infantrymen who marched slowly forward at the Somme paid the same price as the men of Magersfontein. Although British musketry improved, the concept of night attacks, rolling artillery bombardments and the efficiency of rifles in defence all had to be learned the hard way. Once again, the British soldier paid for their officers' inefficiency, but this time in their tens of thousands. With the 1914-1918 horror coming so soon after the campaigns in South Africa, lessons and memories dimmed, although some things passed into popular culture. In the early 1990s, an elderly lady then living in the Scottish Borders scribbled down a skipping rhyme which she said she taught her children during the Second World War. As far as she could recall, the words ran like this:

'The war, the war, the bloomin' war, has turned my wife insane.
From Kruger to Majuba, she's the Transvaal on the brain.
We went to christen our first child, last Sunday week we tried.
The parson said 'What's this child's name?' and my old gal replied:
'The baby's name is Kitchener, Carrington, Methuen, Kekewich,
White, Cronje, Plumer, Powell, Majuba, Gatacre, Warren, Colenso,

*Kruger, Cape Town, Mafeking, French, Kimberley, Ladysmith,
'Bobs', Union Jack, Fighting Mac, Lyddite, Pretoria, Blobbs.'
'The Parson said these names upon this infant I can't pop
So my wife she bruised his rolling veldt and jumped on his Spion
Kop
She kicked his mounted infantry till his Bloemfontein was sore
Then she did a flanking movement and she started out once more.'*

The lady claimed that a slightly more ribald version of the song
had been popular in Music Halls earlier in the century. Perhaps it is
fitting that the game of politicians that cost so many lives should end
in a game of the children whose fathers paid the price.

Yet bitter memories remain, particularly in South Africa. When the
British Prime Minister, Tony Blair, visited South Africa a century
after the last bullet had been fired, Mr J. A Marais, leader of the
Herstige Nasionale Party, the Refounded National Party of South
Africa, demanded that he apologise for the Boer War. 'Is there any
reason why the British Government should not apologise to the
Afrikaner people?'

Perhaps every government should apologise for every war. While
the British were chasing commandos over the veldt, the United
States was fighting its own colonial war in the Philippines. The
Americans had invaded to remove the Spanish presence and
remained to make the Philippines an American colony. The war
lasted until 1914 and between 200,000 and 600,000 Phillipinos died
from disease, famine and direct military action. The German war
against the Hereros between 1904 and 1907 resulted in the
extermination of an estimated 85% of the entire Herero people.

Lieutenant General Lothar von Trotha penned the Herero into a
trap with only the Omaheke Desert as an exit. He then poisoned the
desert water holes, following that with the order "Within the German
borders, every Herero, whether armed or unarmed, with or without
cattle, will be shot. I shall not accept any more women or children. I
shall drive them back to their people - otherwise I shall order shots

147

to be fired at them." Those who survived were worked to death in labour camps. War has always been ugly, and the Boer War was no worse than many another, but still a nightmare for those involved, Briton, Colonial, Boer or native African. In the end it solved nothing, only shifted the problems to another generation. Perhaps some day that simple lesson will be learned.

Malcolm Archibald

Bibliography : Published

Archibald, Malcolm, (1996) *Scottish Animal and Bird Folklore*, (St Andrew Press, Edinburgh)

Brookes, Edgar H & de B Webb, Colin, (1965) *A History of Natal* (University of Natal Press,)

Chandler, David, (General Editor), (1994) *The Oxford Illustrated History of the British Army*, (Oxford University Press)

Conan Doyle, Arthur, (1903) *The Great Boer War*, (Smith and Elder, London)

Creswicke, Louis, (1901) *South Africa and the Transvaal War*, (T.C. & E.C. Jack, Edinburgh

Davidson, Apollon, and Filatova, Irina, (1998) *The Russians and the Anglo-Boer War* (Human & Rousseau)

Dennis, P, Grey, J., Morris, E., Prior, R., and Conney, J., (1995) *The Oxford Companion to Australian Military History* (Oxford University Press, Melbourne)

De Wet, Christiaan Rudolf, *Three Years War*, (1902) (Archibald Constable & Co,)

Dugdale, E.T.S., (translator), (1930) *German Diplomatic Documents, 1871 – 1914*, Volume III *The Growing Antagonism 1898 – 1910* (Harper & Brothers)

Farewell, Byron; (1977) *The Great Boer War*, (Allen Lane)

Field, L., (1979) *The Forgotten War: Australian Involvement in the South African Conflict of 1899 – 1902* (Melbourne University Press, Melbourne)

Gandhi, M. K., (1982) *An Autobiography, or The Story of My Experiments with Truth* (Penguin, London)

Grey, J, (1990) *A Military History of Australia* (Cambridge Press, Melbourne)

Hall, D.O.W., (1949) *The New Zealanders in South Africa 1899-1902* (War History Branch, Wellington)

Haswell, Jock, (1975) *The British Army* (BCA)

Harper, Colonel J. R., (1966) *78th Fighting Frasers: A Short History of the Old 78th Regiment* (Dec-Sco Publications)

Johnson, Paul (editor), (1994) *20th Century Britain: Economic, Social and Cultural Change* (Longman, London)

Kruger, Rayne, (1959) *Good-bye Dolly Gray: The Story of the Boer War.* Cassell, London)

Laband, John, (1997) *The Rise & Fall of the Zulu Nation,* (Arms & Armour Press)

Lynch, Michael, (editor), (2001) *The Oxford Companion to Scottish History* (Oxford, OUP)

MacDonald Fraser, George, (1971) *The Steel Bonnets: The Story of the Anglo-Scottish Border Reivers* (Barrie & Jenkins, London)

McGibbon, I, (1991) *The Path to Gallipoli, Defending New Zealand 1840 – 1915* (GP Books, Wellington)

Maree, D. R., *Bicycles in the Anglo Boer War of 1899 – 1902*, (Military History Journal, Volume 4, No 1 of the South African Military History Society.)

Melville, Michael Leslie, (1981) *The Story of the Lovat Scouts 1900 – 1980* (St Andrew Press, Edinburgh)

Mileham, P. J. R., (1993) *Fighting Highlanders – The History of the Argyll and Sutherland Highlanders,* (Arms and Armour Press)

Morris, Donald R., (1965) *The Washing of the Spears* (Jonathan Cape, London)

Mount, Graeme S., (1993) *Canada's Enemies: Spies and Spying in the Peaceable Kingdom*; (Dundurn Press, Toronto)

Pakenham, Thomas, (1979) *The Boer War*, (Weidenfeld and Nicolson, London)

Plaatje, Sol. T., (1990) *Mafeking Diary: A Black Man's View of a White Man's War.* Ed. John Comaroff with Brian Willan and Andrew Reed. Cambridge, U.K.: (Meridor Books in association with James Currey, London, and Ohio U Press, Athens)

Prebble, John, (1974) *The Lion in the North: A Personal View of Scotland's History*, (BCA)

Pretorius, Fransjohan, (ND) *Life on Commando during the Anglo-Boer War 1899 – 1902* (Human and Roussea, Cape Town,)

Reed, James, (1973) *The Border Ballads* (Athlone Press, London)

Reitz, Deneys, (1929) *Commando,* (Faber & Faber)

Roberts, Andrew, (1999) *Salisbury: Victorian Titan* (Weidenfeld & Nicolson, London)

Selous, F. C., (1893) Travel & Adventure in South-East Africa (Rowland Ward & Co, Limited)

Smith, Iain R., (1996) The Origins of the South African War, 1899-1902. (Longman Group Limited, London and New York)

Spies, S.B., (1977) Methods of Barbarism: Roberts and Kitchener and Civilians in the Boer Republics January 1900 – May 1902 (Human & Rousseau, Cape Town)

Warwick, Peter (ed), (1980) The South African War (The Anglo-Boer War 1899 – 1902) (Longman)

Warwick, Peter, (1983) *Black People and the South African War, 1899-1902.* (Cambridge University Press, Cambridge)

Non Published Sources

Brown, Robert: *Diary*

Donnelly, Douglas: letters and telephone calls to the author

_____